Leslie Schwa

Surviving the Hel ...witz and Dachau

To David

all the best

Leslie Schwartz

20/6/2015

Leslie Schwartz, Marc David Bonagura

Surviving the Hell
of Auschwitz and Dachau

A Teenage Struggle
Toward Freedom From Hatred

LIT

This book is printed on acid-free paper.

Bibliographic information published by the Deutsche Nationalbibliothek
The Deutsche Nationalbibliothek lists this publication in the Deutsche
Nationalbibliografie; detailed bibliographic data are available in the Internet at
http://dnb.d-nb.de.

ISBN 978-3-643-90368-6

A catalogue record for this book is available from the British Library

©LIT VERLAG GmbH & Co. KG Wien,   LIT VERLAG Dr. W. Hopf
Zweigniederlassung Zürich 2013   Berlin 2013
Klosbachstr. 107   Fresnostr. 2
CH-8032 Zürich   D-48159 Münster
Tel. +41 (0) 44-251 75 05   Tel. +49 (0) 2 51-62 03 20
Fax +41 (0) 44-251 75 06   Fax +49 (0) 2 51-23 19 72
E-Mail: zuerich@lit-verlag.ch   E-Mail: lit@lit-verlag.de
http://www.lit-verlag.ch   http://www.lit-verlag.de

Distribution:
In Germany: LIT Verlag Fresnostr. 2, D-48159 Münster
Tel. +49 (0) 2 51-620 32 22, Fax +49 (0) 2 51-922 60 99, E-mail: vertrieb@lit-verlag.de
In Austria: Medienlogistik Pichler-ÖBZ, e-mail: mlo@medien-logistik.at
In Switzerland: B + M Buch- und Medienvertrieb, e-mail: order@buch-medien.ch
In the UK: Global Book Marketing, e-mail: mo@centralbooks.com
In North America: International Specialized Book Services, e-mail: orders@isbs.com
e-books are available at www.litwebshop.de

Contents

FOR MY BELOVED ANNETTE

MY SON GARRY

HALINA KUSTIN JAGENDORF

BEN AND LORRI

IN LOVING MEMORY OF

MY PARENTS – IMRE SCHWARTZ AND MALVIN KOHN

MY SISTER JUDITH

HELEN WEINBERGER

ARTHUR WEINBERGER

AND

CHAIM LAX

Foreword: Creating a Brighter Future

Leslie Schwartz is a man of indomitable spirit. During the torturous days of the Shoah, his will to live was stronger than the Nazi desire to see him die. When it was over, Leslie rebuilt his life in the land of liberty and freedom. He was able to rehabilitate himself physically and emotionally despite the terrible experiences he and his fellow Jews suffered during the war. What drove and inspired him over the years was to see his greatest wish realized: to be able personally to thank the Righteous Gentiles who helped him and saved him in his greatest hour of need.

Leslie has lived to see the birth of a democratic Germany with strong ties to the State of Israel – and as a country that has taken a democracy-loving and promoting leadership role in the post-war European Union. He has been privileged to witness the revival of Jewish life in Germany and Eastern Europe, a revival that was unfathomable just decades ago. He has admirably taken up the cause of Holocaust education, sharing his experiences with non-Jewish European school children.

Having lived through humanity's darkest hour, even as he approaches the sunset of his life, instead of taking it easy and relaxing, Leslie Schwartz continues to travel the globe, dedicating his life to creating a brighter future for us all.

Rabbi Arthur Schneier, Senior Rabbi
Park East Synagogue, New York City

–1–

Introduction: Crucial to the Future

Karen Thisted[1]

In the weeks leading to the unavoidable collapse of what was to be the Thousand Year Reich, the Nazis and their collaborators who knew about the existence of the concentration camps and the fates of the Jews inside them – and those who knew in their hearts that extensive and horrific crimes against humanity had been committed – tried to erase any trace of those crimes by removing as much evidence as they could. They succeeded to some extent, but there were still reminders that could not be destroyed and people who could not be silenced – those were people who managed to escape from the Nazi-created hell.

Approximately one hundred Holocaust survivors die every day, but some voices remain – those who were children and adolescents in the concentration camps. In the past few years, several international coalitions have been established, memorials have been built, museums have been erected, and international conferences held on the subject of the Holocaust. All of this effort is directed toward the purpose of never forgetting that terrible chapter in human history, even as the years pass and the survivors die.

The mass-murder of the Jewish population in Europe by Nazi-Germany during the Second World War has been documented and discussed throughout most of the world. It is the most researched event in human history. Yet, there are still victims of the Holocaust who wish to tell their stories, to bear witness to what happened to their families and to themselves. And now, as those who were children and young adults in the concentration camps are approaching the

---

[1] Karen Thisted is the co-author (with Leslie Schwartz) of *Overleve Helvede* or *Surviving Hell,* the original version of Leslie Schwartz' story, first published in Denmark in January 2007.

end of their lives, they cannot bear the thought of not telling what happened. They feel that telling the world is crucial to the future of humankind.

Leslie Schwartz is one of those child survivors. This book is his story. Now living in New York, Leslie survived four concentration camps: Auschwitz, Dachau, Allach, and Mühldorf. He believes he survived for just one reason: to offer his eye-witness testimony to people around the world. Since the Liberation, whenever and wherever he is able, with a burning passion, Leslie Schwarz does all he can to describe the horrors of the camps. One of the people he told his story to was me.

During his early childhood Leslie was aware of the hatred generated by his government's anti-Jewish policies. As a result of this persecution, when they could, a few hundred thousand German and Eastern European Jews, including members of Leslie's family, fled to foreign countries, primarily the United States – and when Leslie arrived there after the war, they came to mean everything to him.

Hungary was an ally of Germany during the first years of the war. In fact, Hungary fought on the German side during the invasion of the Soviet Union in 1941. This alliance meant that Hungarian Jews met the fate of their less fortunate neighbors, German and Eastern European Jews, at a relatively late date. It was not until 1944, when Germany feared that Hungary would switch sides because of military developments and because they were annoyed at Admiral Horthy's reluctance to deport Hungary's Jews that Germany occupied Hungary on March 19, 1944. From that point on the Nazis were quick to eliminate the Jews of Hungary. Leslie and his family were caught in the massive deportations that took place from May to June 1944. Pushed into cattle cars that crawled through Czechoslovakia to Auschwitz, the death camp in southwestern Poland, they prepared for the worst.

Ten days after his arrival at Auschwitz, Leslie was transferred to Dachau, sixteen kilometers northwest of Munich. The camp, Hitler's first, was established as early as March 20, 1933 to hold political prisoners. It initially held communists, social-democrats, and labor union leaders. The camp commandant was Theodor Eicke, whose particularly brutal methods set the example followed by commandants in the rest of the concentration camps throughout the war.

From 1939-1945, six million Jews were murdered in the concentration camps and ghettos or died from illness and starvation in hiding and in labor camps, in prisons, and from torture. Along with them, large parts of Eastern

European Jewish culture vanished. But that has not stopped the hate. Today, anti-Semitism is starting to blaze anew, especially in Hungary, among all places. Leslie Schwartz says that he, too, is sensing it and that it scares him. He naively thought that after the end of World War II, there would be no more wars, hoping his suffering would be the last.

At a time when discussion about the Holocaust is again gaining resonance, this renewed interest in the subject is especially pronounced in the United States, where Holocaust survivors are telling their stories in many different media. Their testimonies differ from earlier accounts, partly because the people who are telling their stories now have grown bolder and are more open and partly because the spirit of the time demands them to be forthright and vocal.

Albert Einstein, the physicist and human rights advocate, once wrote: "The world is too dangerous to live in – not because of the people who commit evil acts, but because of the people who stand by and let them." Leslie Schwartz knows well these words by Albert Einstein, words containing the essence of his wish to bear witness. He does not want to go to his grave as a bystander.

Romanian-born author and recipient of the Nobel Prize, Professor Elie Wiesel was an inmate in Auschwitz at the same time as Leslie Schwartz. In his book, *Night,* he writes: "Deep down, the witness knew then, as he does now, that his testimony would not be received. After all, it deals with an event that sprang from the darkest zone of man. Only those who experienced Auschwitz knew what it was. Others will never know."

Holocaust is a Greek word, and in the Bible it means "completely burned."

Prologue: Unimaginable Healing

We no longer need to pretend we are all separate. We can indeed face the sometimes brutal but also beautiful greater reality that we are all connected, even related, and that freedom from hatred truly is possible.

I am a Jew – born in Hungary on January 12, 1930. My given name is Laszlo Schwartz, but I am known throughout the world as Leslie. At one time I was even called Lazarus because according to the Christian Bible, Lazarus came back from the dead. I used to think I wasn't supposed to be alive.

At least three times before the age of sixteen, I probably should have died. There is no plausible or rational explanation as to why I lived, except perhaps that even then I was obsessed with telling the rest of the world what I had seen and experienced. I had nightmares that we were all dead – that we all simply disappeared and no one ever knew what happened to us. I had to live to tell my story – a story belonging to so many others perhaps more worthy to speak than I but who did not make it out of hell alive.

I've been told I sometimes echo a detached tone as I relate the details of my life, but this detachment is really a gift. It has allowed me to watch my life like a movie, almost as if I were sitting safely and comfortably in the darkness and anonymity of a theater – just observing all the actors and events – seeking only wisdom. Above all other traits I possess, this ability to observe without judgment has allowed me to heal and to learn the lessons we need to teach future generations.

Remaining bound by hatred and charged emotion serves no greater purpose than to stroke one's ego or put someone else down, and in a very real way, my freedom from hatred has allowed love to flow into formerly closed and barren places in my heart. In a strange and wonderfully ironic manner, this detachment has led to an emotional rebirth –a gathering together of the fragments of my soul in an unbelievable healing experience, something previously thought unimaginable.

Chapter One: Childhood in a Time of War

My father Imre Schwartz had eight siblings, and my Aunt Ida, together with her husband Josef Kuhn, owned a seven-hundred acre farm named Pokahegy about two miles from the Hungarian village of Baktalórántháza where I grew up. The town center is surrounded by fields and woods and farms. I cherished the time I spent at Pokahegy in the summers of my early childhood. Some of my fondest memories are there. My Aunt had horses, cows, and pigs on the farm, and it seemed to me like my family grew almost everything, even tobacco.

Once I arrived, I could eat all I ever wanted. My Aunt served me the most delicious milk, butter, and yogurt, and there were fruit trees of every variety with giant red apples, sweet pears, juicy peaches, and dark cherries. I was also completely fascinated by the bee hives, and I can still hear that zooming buzzing sound. I would stand a few feet away from the hives hypnotized by the vibrations that seemed to move all over my body. I always tried to get the honey inside, but I would usually only get stung and come home with bumps all over my body.

Starting when I was only six or seven years of age, I would leave my mother and father's home in the morning and set out for the two mile journey to the farm. If I were lucky, I'd spend the day there and get back before dark. I was always accompanied by my dog Friend, a German shepherd who went everywhere with me. I remember one summer morning in particular when Friend and I set out for Pokahegy.

The sun is warm on my face, but once we enter the wooded area, the light and warmth fade. The older kids always warn me never to go into the forest alone – there are snakes and bears and even lions, not to mention devils and demons of every description, all waiting to devour me body and soul. Although small for my age, I am one of the fastest runners in my village, at least for short distances, so Friend and I take off dashing through the scary woods.

Picture 1: Ida's husband Josef Kuhn is third from the right with the hat and pipe. American Cousins Ben Gross, left, and David Gross, right.

I want to make it to the farm so badly. The farm is my respite from the stress of my home life. My father is quite stern, and I am a terribly mischievous child, always receiving beatings at his hands. At Pokahegy I can be myself, surrounded by people who love me unconditionally – and all that wonderful food – but first I have to make it through the woods. With Friend by my side, I am not afraid. We keep running faster and faster. Friend leads the way, but on this particular journey we stray from the usual path.

Next to the forest lies the estate and castle of Duke Paul Degenfelt. He is the wealthiest man in town, and he lives just at the edge of the forest. His own armed security force patrols his land. Degenfelt's guards see me and Friend running and start shooting at us, but we keep running.

I am almost there, but I'm getting tired. I can only run fast for short distances, so I stop for a moment to catch my breath when we are past the guards' line of sight. I hug Friend and feel her fur to see if she is all right, but she has been shot near her belly. I feel the warm blood on her beautiful fur. Now fear totally grips me. She licks my face. We get up and start running again. We have to keep running – we must make it to my Aunt's farm so I can get help for Friend.

Completely exhausted, I'm now running in slow motion, like in dreams, with every step and every breath a struggle. Even though I am surrounded by danger, I know safety and comfort await me at my Aunt's farm. I have only a short distance to go. I have to make it to save Friend. Everyone is waiting for us when we arrive. With my Aunt Ida's first aid, Friend survives the shooting, my Aunt's farm and her genuine kindness always a safe haven against the brutality of the world.

I am the child of a disabled man. My father was stricken with polio when he was sixteen and crippled for the rest of his life. He was a talented but strict man who owned a small retail shop that sold mostly cosmetics, beauty crèmes, and lotions. He was especially adept at making perfumes. I always watched everything he did very closely. He often took me with him when he bought the essential oils used in his secret formulas from which he created the fragrances. I just thought he was brilliant.

My father was self-taught in all his passions and pursuits. He loved music and played the violin so beautifully that I grew up thinking God went out of His way to bestow gifts on the handicapped. In addition to his other talents, he was also an exceptional photographer and painter. I was never embarrassed by the fact that everyone in town recognized him as he walked along so slowly with his cane. The townsfolk considered him a genius too because he acted as lecturer and advisor to all the local peasants. No one ever cared that he wasn't like everyone else.

My father came from an upper middle-class family and was brought up well, so despite his disability, he was still able to marry a beautiful, wise wo-man – my mother, Malvin Kohn. Though their marriage was arranged, they got along well enough to have two children, my younger sister Judith and me. We were two years apart and very attached to each other. Maybe that was because we created a united front in the face of my father, a tough disciplinarian in the old-fashioned, European kind of way. My father simply had to have everything his way, and I was often the target of his wrath.

When you're a child and your father hits you, however else you might interpret that action, it signals interest in you – and for me, even such pro-

*Picture 2: Leslie's immediate family in 1933;
from left to right, his mother, Malvin Kohn,
grandfather, Samuel Schwartz, and father, Imre
Schwartz*

blematic and uncomfortable attention had great value. I realize this point may be difficult to explain, but even though he beat me, I always knew my father cared deeply about me and that what I did mattered a great deal to him. I can say quite honestly I would have felt much worse had he ignored me. In fact, the passion and directness of a blow instantly reminded me of the constant attention he seemingly paid to every minute detail of my life.

In short, he wanted me to be a good person and a good Jew – and he would stand for nothing less than my complete attention. When we were at the synagogue together, almost every day, I sat close to him and paid careful attention to my prayers. If I so much as glanced the other way, he would give me a scolding and a slap.

I now believe my father was also training me to be mentally and physically tough – the times required that, but even more importantly, like he knew on some level that his son needed to be very strong, almost immune to physical punishment and mental anguish to survive what was to come – and that he only had a short time to deliver this message to me.

In any event I was very proud of him because he was unusual and people always came to him for advice. Even our Christian neighbors turned to him when they had problems with the authorities or problems of a private nature; this service he generously offered meant we had many friends.

I was the youngest of my crew of friends by at least two years and wanted nothing more than to spend time with them; there were three older boys in particular whom I practically worshipped. Initially, they didn't want me around because I was so young and looked even smaller for my age, but I didn't give up so easily. They were always having fun, and I wanted to be part of their clique.

Because of my father's business, I was usually able to earn a bit of money that I could use to bribe my way into the group. They always said to me, "Go home and get more money!" And I did, although it wasn't ever quite enough. Since I also worked in my father's shop, I had access to a line of credit with a local store that sold chocolate and ice-cream, further helping to facilitate my acceptance with the older boys.

As I write this in 2012, we are all still alive – imagine that! Two of us live in Canada, Bela Lowy in Toronto and Endre Grosz in Montreal, Sandor Feldman lives in Brooklyn, and I live in Manhattan. We all had many childhood adventures back when life was still normal in Baktalórántháza.

Most Saturdays we would trek through the nearby woods, and one day we met a Gypsy woman. She wore a dress over heavy pants, yet she walked barefoot. She also carried a large walking stick and had various bags and pouches strung over her shoulders filled with plants she had gathered deep in the forest. Her dark hair fell down in front of her face in long braids.

She scared the life out of me as she seemed to appear out of thin air, stepping out from behind a huge tree. I was the youngest and smallest, so the older boys pushed me forward, forcing me to stand right in front of her. They were having a good laugh, but I was terrified. I couldn't even move. She seemed to read me like a book. Then she spoke to me, "Whoever gives me money, the Devil will not take!"

I had a few pennies in my pocket, so I willingly gave her what I had. We saw her several times after that. I wasn't scared of her anymore, but I always gave her my pennies.

These older boys allowing me into their circle really solidified my sense of belonging and safety. Additionally, the love and attention I received from my father though rough was quite palpable and always consistent. As far as I knew, my life at eight years of age seemed rock solid and secure.

One day the door to my classroom in the Jewish primary school opened. Without warning a stranger walked purposefully into the room. I looked up from my little desk.

He looked straight at me, speaking with no emotion, "Laszlo Schwartz, come on home. Your father is dead."

At that time in the Jewish religion, it was customary to put the deceased in a room in his house, cover the body with a sheet, and light candles all around him, and this ritual was an awful experience for me because my bedroom was now right next door to the room that housed my dead father. Everyone expected me to fall asleep and behave normally, but I was terrified. At the funeral all I wanted to do was jump into the grave and go with him. I just didn't want to live without him. That was 1938.

My father died from Tuberculosis. He always seemed so incredibly strong to me, but I'm sure he was weakened by the Polio he suffered in his youth, and his body could not fight off the ravages of the Consumption. In the short time that I knew him, he gave me so much. One of the attributes he instilled in me was the desire to live a life of integrity and honesty.

Shortly before he died, my father experienced the effects of the persecution of the Jews in a small, yet personal way. The highlight of my father's life was to play the violin while his friend played the clarinet. Every Thursday the two of them would give classical concerts in our home and finish the session with a delicious dinner prepared by my mother – she was a fantastic cook by the way. But one Thursday his friend did not come and gave no explanation. We never saw him again.

Being a child I didn't fully understand what happened, but I saw my father's world darken, and this incident, although relatively minor in comparison with all we would soon go through, left a lasting impression on me. His friend had joined the Nazi party. My father never spoke much about it, but his thinly veiled sorrow and obvious despair were quite evident to me. This was my first memory of the coming Holocaust.

While I was still trying to recover from the loss of my father, I learned that my mother was going to marry a man named Josef Romer. This too was an arranged marriage. I was then nine years old, and from the very beginning I didn't like Romer. I realized that my mother would never have been able to care properly for Judith and me if she hadn't remarried, but she also seemed so much happier with her new husband, and this bothered me even more.

In some Jewish family traditions, including my family's, children are not permitted to attend a parent's wedding to a new partner, so on top of everything else, the fact that I was barred from attending the ceremony absolutely infuriated me. I took Judith with me, and we hid in the gardens in back of our house. Judith did not understand my anger, but in that moment I wished to disappear forever into the green void of the plants and trees.

By the time Romer broke the glass under the wedding canopy, I was so completely repulsed by him that I kept my distance whenever possible, often childishly ignoring him. I just felt betrayed by everyone. In a way, this mistrust of Romer later saved my life – for if I had loved him and trusted completely in his judgment, I would have perished along with the rest of the Jews who went up in smoke at Auschwitz. There were, however, other consequences to my attitude.

As for my mother, I felt that she was unfaithful to the memory of my father by remarrying so quickly. I sensed a distance develop between us that had never before existed – if I had only known how precious little time I had left to spend with her, I would have swallowed my pride in a heartbeat. I was so angry about Romer's place in my family that I even directed some of that rage at my half-sister Eva, who was born in 1943. I was so unattached to her that I have difficulty remembering almost anything about her.

As a result of my attitude, there was even talk of sending me to stay with relatives in the United States. It came so close, but it never happened. In addition to the betrayal my father suffered, another early memory of the impending Holocaust was the closing of our school.

One day we attended classes in the Jewish primary school, and the next day it was closed and our teachers sent away – they simply disappeared. We were then ordered to report to the local Roman Catholic school where I found myself, quite noticeably, in the minority among a large group of Catholic children.

Sharing this school was a strange and awkward circumstance indeed. The Catholics were as uncomfortable with us as we were with them. The superstitions about our respective religions cut both ways, and while they were hostile to Judaism, we were hostile to Christianity. It didn't help that during religion class the Jewish children were sent outside. That made us seem even more mysterious to our non-Jewish classmates, and when they were taught that we Jews killed Jesus, we knew things could not possibly get better.

During this time period, the late 1930s through early 1940s, the gap between my non-Jewish friends and neighbors and my family grew wider and wider, and people with whom we had formerly been very close suddenly wouldn't have anything to do with us as they were bombarded with hate-filled propaganda. This rising tide of anti-Semitism really took us by surprise because Hungarian Jews were otherwise very well-integrated.

I considered myself a patriotic citizen of the Hungarian nation. There was no doubt about that in my mind. All the Jews in my town were patriots. We took an interest in anything that had to do with Hungary and always rooted for the Hungarian sports teams. But suddenly I was no longer a part of Hungarian society. Now I was a *dirty Jew* whatever that meant. That's how the Hungarian authorities portrayed us. I started to feel increasingly self-conscious and defensive. Whenever I passed by the Roman Catholic church, I was so scared I walked as fast as I could, without running, because if anyone saw me running, I thought they might shout, "Look at that little Jewish boy – he spits at the crucifix!"

In only a few short years every aspect of my world had been turned upside down, from my family life to my place among my friends and neighbors in the community. Even the way I saw myself had changed. I began to doubt my self-worth and importance. But even then I had the resiliency to survive in difficult circumstances, to make the best of life no matter what.

The teacher's daughter, Judith Pocz – I still remember her name – was the loveliest girl at school and perhaps the first to inspire my lifelong fascination with beauty despite all the ugliness surrounding me.

Judith was eight years old, and I was completely infatuated with her. I was in so deep that I still remember her angelic face and how beautifully she was always dressed, but to me her best feature was her wavy, brown hair. She seemed to be continually combing and brushing it, and I watched her in complete fascination. My obsession with her took over my thoughts allowing me to forget about the hate for a short time anyway.

We slipped each other little notes, and she was absolutely aware that I liked her, but her mother had to be kept in the dark as both she and her husband had joined the Nazi party and told Judith in no uncertain terms that she was not to associate with me.

Whenever my teacher left the classroom to do an errand, she would appoint a "good" student to watch the rest of us and to write the names of those who misbehaved on the blackboard. My name was constantly written on the board

Picture 3: Leslie Schwartz, second row, fifth from right (directly in front of the girl with the white blouse and dress that resembles suspenders) and his Catholic school classmates, 1940. Judith Pocz, third row, fourth from the right (to the immediate right of the girl with the suspenders).

because I was always busy drawing attention to myself so that Judith would notice me. As far as I could tell, I was in love with her until they sent us Jews away – completely away.

Chapter Two: Deportation

In the years immediately following my father's death, Hungary passed three major anti-Jewish laws, the last one in 1941 modeled after Germany's "race protective" Nuremberg Laws. In essence, the rights associated with our citizenship were gradually taken away. All I could understand of these laws as a boy was that anyone who was not a Hungarian citizen was not going to be able to make a living and sooner or later at great risk of being deported, but I certainly could not comprehend how my family and I could fall into the category of non-citizens. My grandparents were born in Hungary, so how could the Government claim we were not Hungarian? Yet we were already living in such a hateful atmosphere, I often wondered if we might actually be better off leaving.

Then one day in January 1943 it happened. The local government officials ordered us to show up at the train station for what would become a prelude to later events. All of the Jews in my village were surprised that winter morning when police officers came and picked us up. They told us to pack only what we were able to carry and some food. I was out in the courtyard with Friend when my mother called for me.

My family and I were taken to the train station, and along with us, many other Jews from our town were packed into railroad cattle cars. Little did I know how horribly familiar these cattle transport wagons would become. We had only the food we brought with us, no water, and a single bucket for human waste. And there was no heat inside the wooden cars. We heard we were going to Ukraine. Sometimes we stopped along the way and a few decent people took pity on us and brought us water. The way I remember it, we rode on the train for about a day, stopping near the Hungarian-Ukrainian border.

The train stopped in a very beautiful area with picturesque snow-capped mountains in the background. Our guards handed us blankets, and I began to feel like I was on a primitive camping trip. We waited in those mountains for a few days, with barely anything to eat or drink, when suddenly the orders changed.

The Russians were advancing and had closed the border with Ukraine, and the Hungarian authorities then decided that we would be sent back to our town. Maybe it was because the Nazis and Hungarian sympathizers didn't want the Russians to see what they were doing to the Jews, or maybe it was simply because they were at war with each other. Whatever the reason, we were lucky. We cheated death. We were brought back to our town, yet everyone knew the deported never returned, especially from where we had been sent, a literal killing fields for Jews during the war.

I learned from other survivors that during this time period our fellow Hungarians also lined up Jews on banks of the Danube or at the edges of large pits and simply shot them as they fell into reddened waters and pits, mass-graves they were forced to dig themselves. Back during that time period, without any confirmation, we also heard other rumors of mass murder, even that the Nazis were packing people into ships and sinking them in the Black Sea.[2]

Most of the Nazi collaborators in the occupied countries behaved as badly as the worst of the Germans; they seized every opportunity to commit horrendous crimes against their former friends and neighbors, and being home again meant that we now had no more friends or allies of any kind. Still, we tried to resume our lives back in Baktalórántháza as if nothing unusual had ever happened.

But as time passed, the anti-Semitic propaganda only increased. In my village, posters went up that described us in horrible terms, saying Jews were something less than animals. To add injury to insult, one winter day in 1944, the local police went to every Jewish household and demanded that we hand over all our gold, silver, and precious stones. I was fourteen when I watched my mother give them her wedding ring and the rest of the family's jewelry. I'll

---

[2]   The *SS Struma*, packed with Jews, had been chartered to take its passengers to Mandate Palestine. The engine broke, and after being marooned in the Bosphorus, while waiting for the British to grant them permission to dock in Haifa, the Turks towed the ship back to the Black Sea. A Russian submarine torpedoed the boat on February 23, 1942 and drowned 768 Jews. One survived. Another shipload of deportees from Thrace was sunk at the end of March or beginning of April 1943. It was one of four Bulgarian ships taking 4,226 Jews to Auschwitz. It is unclear whether or not it was deliberately sunk. Another ship, the *Mefkura*, was one of three German-approved shipments of Jews headed for Mandate Palestine in August 1944. It was sunk when it was fired upon by an unknown vessel. There were only five survivors.

never forget seeing our watches and rings and other valuable items spread out on our dining table.

Everything was confiscated except for my grandfather's prized possession. It was a beautiful and precious pocket watch given to him by his children in America, and it was not on the table. My mother had carefully packed it away without telling any of us so that it could be left with our neighbors. She was so brave. She wanted to stash things away for when life would one day return to normal. She believed with all her heart that our Christian neighbors, the Paps, could be trusted to safeguard grandfather's watch for when the good times returned. I always felt comfortable at the Pap's home and had no reason to doubt my mother's plan.

I spent a great deal of time with my neighbors – they had a boy named Janos who was about my age. I loved the food I would get over there, especially roasted pork, bacon, and ham, all of which were forbidden in my home. One Christmas they were roasting a pig in their fireplace hearth. I climbed into it and ripped off a huge piece of meat. Everyone quickly figured out who was responsible for the missing meat. I got a good beating when I returned home.

It was just after Passover 1944 when our nightmares became reality. Being a highly curious boy, I simply had to know what was going on, and I could tell something was really wrong. My mother gathered us around the dinner table and said quietly: "We have to leave our home. I don't know for how long." Then she pulled me aside and told me, as the oldest child, that she had given grandfather's watch to the Paps.

My mother seemed to know what was coming and tried her best to prepare us. She was very friendly with the town's postmaster. He'd learned that all the Jews were soon to be taken from the town and warned my mother two days before the deportations began. It was a brave act that could have cost him his life.

For two days before our expulsion, she cooked and baked for our journey. She packed it all as though preparing for a party. The next day the police knocked on our door, just as they had a year earlier, and ordered us to line up in front of the synagogue. They told us we could bring whatever we were able to carry.

My own emotions were quite mixed as I had heard the grown-ups talking about the deportations. I was neither child nor adult, and while I sensed uncertainty, as a fourteen-year-old I was also somewhat excited. For a long time we had been miserable, but now what? Might this be a change for the better?

Walking from door to door, the police were ordering all Jews outside. I took as much clothing as I could carry, and out the door we went. The front door remained open. As we walked away, Friend was looking at me with her sad eyes, standing in our doorway as if to guard our home until we returned. She first tried to follow us but I begged her to stay. I left her behind for the last time when we marched to the synagogue. My whole family stepped in time as the officers yelled:

"One."

"Two."

"Three."

"Four."

When we got to the synagogue, we saw all the Jewish families in town lined up in the courtyard. All my friends were there, surrounded by their belongings and looking very scared on what was a sunny and beautiful morning. Summer was just around the corner, but there we all were – crying and bickering as the guards rained down threats upon us: "If you don't do as you are told, we will shoot you right here!"

Everyone was confused, wondering what was going to happen next, and then I witnessed something truly unusual – a mass of cattle-drawn ox-carts moving slowly through the streets, the hooves of the cattle clip-clopping along, all converging on the synagogue courtyard. They had come to take us away. Nazi propaganda was so powerful, so immensely efficient, that scores of local farmers, following orders, arrived in their oxcarts to transport their former friends and neighbors to their deaths.

We were so frightened that we entered those carts ourselves, each one cart holding six or seven people. I don't remember anyone resisting. We were terrified and humiliated to the point of paralysis. This paralysis was dream-like and awful, and I will never forget it. It was inconceivable how they managed to instill such fear. I cannot explain it. It truly seemed like the Nazi effort to bring us down was succeeding in every possible way.

In the months before we were deported, we woke up each day to face new propaganda attacks. Flyers were nailed to trees, hung from street lamps, and posted on walls reading: "Dirty Jews, what are you doing here?" And "Jews are dirty beasts." I even started to think truthfully I was nothing but a "dirty Jew." I felt very alone with my thoughts, and that isolation allowed enough self-doubt for me to believe the lies.

There was so much unbearable hatred toward us even before we ever boarded those oxcarts. Although I had experienced my father's death six years before, it was then at the age of fourteen on that sunny day in May that I first felt genuine sorrow. My mother, stepfather, two sisters, Judith and Eva, a couple of young cousins, and I were all packed into one of the oxcarts to begin our journey out of Baktalórántháza. Out of the corner of my eye, I saw a poster nailed to a tree in front of the synagogue. In capital letters it read: NOW WE ARE RID OF THE JEWS.

After the oxcarts left the synagogue courtyard and rumbled along the road, all the church bells in town suddenly rang out. My mother looked at me so sadly. The carts moved slowly through the streets as if following some gruesome parade route for our grand exit. I certainly did not think I would ever return to Baktalórántháza.

We were taken down to the railroad station and packed for the second time in a year into box-like wooden railroad cars, designed to transport cattle to the slaughterhouses, and after riding in similarly deplorable conditions for hours, the train finally stopped.

All of us were then led to the Jewish ghetto in Kisvarda – only seventeen miles from Baktalórántháza. This trip would normally take half an hour. That day it was stretched out, all part of a carefully designed plan to demoralize and humiliate us. Everything was planned down to the smallest detail.

The families who lived in the ghetto were forced to give us rooms, and we were assigned to a very religious family. We unpacked our things along with the food my mother had prepared and packed so carefully. They had their own food. We all ate our meals in their kitchen in complete silence. We were strangers, yet forced to live together.

I spent most of my days there looking for people I knew from our town. As it turned out, we stayed in the ghetto for a month The days passed slowly. We ate the food my mother had brought. Eventually there was no more. I remember her standing in the unfamiliar kitchen trying to make something out of onions and potatoes.

We did not speak much with the family who owned the apartment because we felt more comfortable with the people we knew, like the Rabbi from our town, Chaim Silber. He was in his mid-sixties and not in the best of health, but he was an extremely nice man who tried to keep our spirits up. I also passed time with my clique. We snuck around the courtyards, but never ever talked about escaping or resisting.

We were so scared the entire time and kept asking the SS officers who were running things what was going to happen. They told us, "You don't have to be afraid. Everything will be all right. Soon we will move you to a place where you will work and get paid and have a normal life." These assurances did not lessen our fears because there was always the unspoken threat that if we did anything wrong, we would be shot. None of us doubted that. How terrifying to know that we could be dead in a moment, not just from the Germans, but from our fellow Hungarians – all this in our own country, among our own people.

I was so young that I still found it difficult to understand how everyone could hate us so much. Up until at least five, six years ago, we had lived peaceful lives together. But the Nazis could achieve anything they wanted by using propaganda. Their ugly words and lies worked like magic. They turned us into enemies of our countrymen. They claimed that Jews were shrewder than others and made more money and were more successful in business. But now that would all end.

During the time we spent in the ghetto, a successful and wealthy man from my hometown died. This man we had always called "Lucky," because everything always went his way. The man was not yet fifty years old when he died from a virus in the ghetto. We all envied him, even without consciously knowing what horrors awaited us.

To prepare his body for proper burial, the deceased was placed in a standing position and carefully rinsed with water. During this ritual, Sandor Grosz, the older brother of Endre Grosz from my group of friends, stood and watched. I'll never forget what Sandor said as he looked around at all of us: "My God! When the lucky man dies here – he who has been lucky his whole life – then we are really looking at some bad times to come."

Chapter Three: Journey to Hell

Although my family and I had been spared when the first waves of deportations were stopped almost as they had begun, within a year's passing the political and social climate had completely degenerated. This time there would be no coming home and no aborted attempts at genocide. When the Arrow Cross Party, the Hungarian fascists, took over the government, they quickly began implementing the Final Solution.

The mass deportations in Hungary started on May 15, 1944 and continued for approximately ten weeks. Within that time frame perhaps a half million or more Hungarian Jews, including myself and my family, were taken to Auschwitz-Birkenau.

I remember the day we left the ghetto once and for all. It was not yet light out, and the SS Guards were already screaming at us. I felt like a scared little boy again, rushing to find my mother and hold her hand. I carried a backpack filled with some clothes we thought we would need, all the while the SS Guards barked out:

"Get ready – march!"

"Eins."

"Zwei."

"Drei."

"Vier!"

In our small area we were seven hundred Jews, marching in confusion and carrying our odd-looking baggage. My mother had to march carrying my sister Eva in her arms.

What was most unsettling to me was that only two SS officers oversaw the entire march, both of whom looked to be no more than seventeen or eighteen years old. They were dressed in fancy uniforms that made them look very powerful. They used their rifles and cudgels to beat the older Jews who were unable to walk fast enough. I stared at them, wondering how was it possible for two boys with German shepherds and weapons to scare the life out of seven hundred Jews?

When we came to the railway station, we were once again forced into railroad cattle cars. When I saw how we were to travel, I did not cry or scream or display any outward emotion. I did not resist in any way. I did not say anything to anyone. I simply stepped into the disgusting train and stayed close to my mother and my family. We stayed together the whole trip. All the while I knew deep in my gut that something was seriously wrong – that terrible things were going to happen.

I can still hear the sound of the locks clanging shut after they slid the doors closed on us – as if we were indeed cattle on the way to a slaughterhouse. And just like that we were off. We rode and rode and rode and rode – for five days immersed in the stench of human waste. The cattle cars were like square wooden boxes on wheels – completely dark inside, except for the light that streamed through small spaces between the wooden planks.

The fear we initially experienced is more than I can accurately describe. This terror gripped us even before they slammed the sliding doors shut. It was like taking a deep breath without being allowed to exhale; the emotion flooded our cells with no possibility of release. Everyone was so tightly wrapped in this terror, and we knew there was no one in the world that could save us now.

There were between seventy to one hundred people in my car. I tried to find peepholes, openings in the wooden planks, so I could look out, but I was not tall enough to reach any.

With each day the journey became more unbearable. We settled ourselves in a corner of the car because sitting in the middle was far worse. There was no toilet, and nothing had been done to spare us humiliation. My mother saved the food as well as she could, but after a day there was nothing left. At different times people panicked, becoming hysterical and screaming to be let out. I begged my mother to make them stop.

I was drifting in and out of a fitful sleep, and I thought I was dreaming when the wheels of the train finally ground to a stop. It was midnight when the gates of the cattle car opened. Then I heard shouting.

"Come on – faster!"

"Faster!"

"Faster!"

I was cold and moving very slowly because I had just woken up. The Nazis held batons for beating us and were intent on getting us out of those cars quickly. Still groggy, I watched as our beloved Rabbi Silber who could not keep up the pace demanded by his tormentors was beaten mercilessly. The small children cried constantly. Everything was dark. We had no idea where we were. Once outside, as raindrops hit my face, I realized this was not a terrifying dream, and I could not wait to get away from that train, as if somehow that would end the horror.

"Out!"

"Out!"

"Out!"

The railroad car stood on the platform at the center of a large junction. Additional SS officers jumped onto the train, beating and yelling at the people still inside the car. We then scattered in every direction. I felt dizzy. Everything slowed down for me, and suddenly I saw this huge flame. I knew they were doing something evil with that flame – that it represented completely insanity. Then an order sounded, snapping me back into my tired body and the present moment.

"Leave everything – out!"

As we moved away from the cars, everyone looked terrified as a clamorous noise echoed all around us. I then realized this journey was efficiently designed to destroy us mentally, tear down our humanity, trample our spirit, and convince us that we were worth nothing. I must say that the Nazis succeeded in every way. This place was where we truly learned to understand hopelessness. All the belongings we dragged with us from home were left on the train.

We had indeed arrived at Auschwitz. In front of us was the concentration camp – a gigantic complex encompassing many different camps, among them Birkenau, Monowitz, and Stammlager. The mass killings of the Hungarian Jews were about to reach their peak. Several thousand arrived just on the day we stepped off the train, and by the end of the war more than a million Jews from all around the world would die here in Auschwitz.

My destiny was first decided on that platform, where the initial selection took place. Women, children, and the elderly were sent to one line, men to another, but I was in between a boy and a man – though I knew I looked small for my age.

I could not make up my mind. Should I follow my mother who was carrying the baby and had Judith by her side? Should I hold her hand and go with her? Should I join my stepfather?

I still did not trust my stepfather, yet I thought it would be best to join the

Picture 4: The railroad platform at Auschwitz, May 1944.

men. My mother's line smelled of dread and trepidation. I had a feeling that something was not right on that line. That special feeling, my sense of inner-knowing, which came and went at different times, is probably what saved me, again and again, through this horrific odyssey.

I went back to my mother's line – back and forth – back and forth. I became more and more desperate and more and more indecisive.

I should just stay with my mother.

I had to make a choice. My mother's line started to move ahead faster and faster. All at once I lost sight of her, Judith, and little Eva. They were gone. We never got a chance to say goodbye or exchange last words or anything. I could not believe it had happened that fast.

In the midst of thinking *maybe I still have time to join her line and find her again* something clicked in my brain. I made the decision to go with my

Picture 5: Women and children at Auschwitz, May 1944.

stepfather. I finally had strength enough to make a choice, and in that moment any choice, real or perceived, offered me hope that I still had some measure of control over whether I lived or died. He and I were then jogging along on the men's line, so I became a man.

After I decided to stay with the men, I witnessed some of the worst crimes I would see during my journey through the camps as the line of women and children was clearly visible from our line. Screams echoed through the air each time an SS officer grabbed a little girl's arm and tore her away from her mother. Their high-pitched screams would not cease as mothers and children were ripped from each other's arms. I saw it all. I saw them being pulled away from each other, but I too was helpless. There was nothing I could do, and I did nothing.

Suddenly, I was separated from my stepfather and stood facing a man that I later learned was the infamous Doctor Josef Mengele. He was gauging our abilities. Mengele was also looking for interesting subjects, especially twins, for his ghastly medical experiments. This selection took place in an open field.

Everything was muddy, dirty, and cold, and the whole time all I could hear was order after order ringing through the air:

"Left!"

"Right!"

"Left!"

"Right!"

When Doctor Mengele saw me, he grabbed my arms and felt my muscles – "How old are you?"

"Seventeen."

I lied so fast that I had no time to be scared. But being small and skinny, I knew I did not look seventeen. I stood there humbly, letting him feel my muscles. Oddly, he impressed me. A handsome man in his thirties, he wore a dapper military uniform. I was truly fascinated by him. He seemed so emotionally detached from everything that was happening all around him, almost as if he were above it all – as if his decisions were completely removed from all human considerations and feelings, like we were all just machines to be taken apart and inspected.

As my attention wandered from Mengele, I tried to look for my mother.

Further down, I could see the row of women and children – and I could still hear their sobs and cries. I wondered if I had been wrong not to go with her. I was confused again. Had I done the right thing?

After a little while, we were once again on the move, this time off to the showers. We handed over all our clothes and put them in a pile. Barbers cut off our hair while we stood there naked. The only thing left on my head was a row of hair an inch long, in the style of a prisoner – instantly recognizable in case we escaped. They even shaved off my pubic hair and the hair on my arms and legs. All the hair that landed on the floor was pushed into huge piles.

"Next."

"Next."

"Next."

Observing this bizarre ritual were the Polish Jewish men who had been at the camp for years. They were kapos, monitors assigned to watch the newcomers. I would learn later that was an attractive job. Kapos ate better food than the inmates and got special treatment. But in the end it didn't matter. They too were murdered.

We were then taken to be assigned prison uniforms. The guards looked us over and guessed what size we were. The uniforms were made of harsh striped wool, and they were stored on shelves, sorted neatly by size. People with eye glasses had to hand them over. The glasses were put in large piles.

So there we were naked, shivering, miserable, and defenseless, putting on our prison garb. Some uniforms were too large, others too small, so we would swap. Each of us also received a cap and a pair of clogs, like the ones worn in Holland. We had no socks, and it was very cold despite the season.

All this time I noticed a bizarre smell hovering everywhere. There was no escape from it. The air smelled charred, burnt like ashes, but with a foul, nauseating odor. Much later I realized I was smelling burned human flesh and only then did I incredulously connect the evil flame that greeted me on the platform to the murder of the Jews.

After we received our uniforms, the kapos directed us back to our barracks.

Doctor Mengele had sent me off to the children's hut, number 13, and I did not like this situation one bit. Once inside, I became despondent, I was truly lonely. I had horrible thoughts and felt really sorry for myself. For the first time since I arrived at Auschwitz, I cried. I felt completely alone not wanting to associate with these other strange children. I knew I was in great danger if I stayed there.

In my misery I soon discovered that we could move around the camp.

They were not afraid we would escape as there was barbed wire everywhere. I found someone from back home and told him how sad I was to have been placed in the children's barracks. There was nothing he could do about it.

The next morning I went outside, hoping, like almost every day I spent in the concentration camps, to find my mother and my sisters. I discovered that the women and children were on the other side of an electrically-charged fence. Every time I saw a woman's back, I thought it was my mother.

While I looked everywhere, I was getting very hungry because we had nothing to eat since we arrived at the camp more than twelve hours ago. You might think we'd lose our appetites in a place like that, but that's not how the human body works. I was starving, and while searching for something to eat, I happened upon my stepfather, Romer. I told him how sad I was to be with the kids, but he said, "It is best for you to stay there. The children are safer." Although I did not like him, I asked, "Shouldn't I rather come with you?" He paused and simply said, "No, stay with the children – it's best for you."

He was under the illusion that Nazis had more heart when it came to children; he believed you were guaranteed survival if you were placed among the kids, but I felt that if I stayed with them, I would die. For the time being I had no alternative than to return to barrack number 13 to get something to eat.

Later that afternoon, my first meal inside a concentration camp was soup made from horsemeat – served in a can that six people shared. The diet remained the same the entire time we were there. You took a sip from the can and passed it on to the next person. I did not think about the taste. I was hungry, and this was how we ate. Nothing else mattered.

In the mornings they gave us black coffee. Previously, I could not drink coffee without milk, but it did not matter now. We ate and drank anything they gave us and anything that we could get our hands on, even if it was lying on the ground and disgusting or if it stank from decay or even if it was hidden under someone else's mattress.

Chapter Four: Brutal Universe

I wanted to be strong, so I felt I needed to despise those who cried out from hunger or longing or grief. When they yelled that dying would be merciful, I truly hated them. I tried hard to maintain this toughened mental attitude. I believed, especially in very beginning of my imprisonment, that I needed to channel all the hatred I could muster for energy to fuel my survival, and I certainly did not feel much sympathy for anyone. I couldn't stand to see people give away their bread in exchange for cigarettes. They died quickly. Everyone who smoked died because they would rather have cigarettes than food. I never pitied the weak prisoners either, those who gave up and let themselves be beaten to death on the ground.

After a little more than a week at Auschwitz, I came to the realization that I wasn't going to survive much longer on my own. I needed an ally. I had once seen Sandor Grosz from my hometown around the yard, so I started looking for him again. Back home, we were not friends because I was just a little kid to him. But now I hoped Sandor might see me in a different light.

Despite my small physical stature, I was banking on the fact that our recent shared trauma might have earned me some respect in Sandor's eyes and perhaps he would help me in some way because right next to the thought that I needed to become insensitive and brutal to survive and that hatred would be the best fuel to feed that process was the contradictory notion that we all needed to help each other to get through this trial – but would love truly hold more power than hate? Mirroring the war all around us, these opposing ideas constantly battled for control of my heart and mind.

I found Sandor standing in line while waiting for my prisoner number. One of the prisoners was in charge of distributing the numbers. He managed the job without displaying the slightest emotion, as though he were merely employed in an office. As expected, in the German fashion, everything was well-organized. Red numbers were for political prisoners. I got a red number, though I didn't understand why. After ten days in Auschwitz, I was no longer Laszlo Schwartz – I was now 71253.

By now I had stopped looking for my stepfather. I never saw him again. Without Sandor I'd have been truly alone, yet later that same day Sandor told me he was being sent to a different camp the next morning. Once back in the childrens's barracks, realizing Sandor was my only possible ally, I kept repeating softly to myself, while sitting with my head down and my eyes closed, "Sandor Grosz is being transferred to a labor camp in the morning."

I looked up scornfully at the other kids my age playing outside. Next to losing my mother and sisters, this was probably one of my worst moments in Auschwitz. I thought those children did not have a clue about what was really going on, and at the same time I was sad that I simply could not just become one of them.

The next morning before dawn I snuck out of the children's barracks and mixed in with the grown men marching toward the train station. The morning light was just rising. Suddenly a German voice yelled from the loudspeakers. Everything became quiet. I was standing next to Sandor

"Achtung!" "Achtung!"

"Number 71253 – where are you?"

Sandor and I froze as the others kept moving around us.

"Now they're going to kill me," I said.

"Yes," he replied simply.

Then a miracle happened. The train arrived. People suddenly began pushing and shoving their way toward the tracks. Amid this chaos in the dim light and mist of that summer morning, I was able to slip right through the crowd, and I was one of the first to climb aboard. A sense of relief ran through me when the train began to move. Again, I was talking quietly to myself, eyes closed, repeating, "Everything will soon be all right. Everything will soon be all right. Everything will soon be all right."

The train was full of men – no women and no children. Men were going to work. I was with Sandor Grosz and stayed close to him the whole trip. It was the beginning of a life-long friendship.

On the way to Dachau, we had been promised a better life, and we were treated a bit better on the train. They fed us, not much, but some. We were to be part of the work force and could not be too weak. I had lost a lot of weight during the past couple weeks, but always did my best to appear able-bodied.

After a two-day journey, the train stopped. From the sign at the station,

I knew we had arrived at Dachau. As we passed through the town center on the way to the concentration camp, I noticed it was a nice little town. The fact that I was even able to have a positive thought was probably because I was no longer in Auschwitz.

Dachau turned out to be a way station. Two days later we were ordered to climb aboard a convoy of trucks heading due south to a camp near Munich called Allach. It was a small camp compared to Auschwitz and Dachau, but the barracks looked alike in all three camps, and, in truth, the conditions in all three camps were still wretched. The humiliation and beatings were also the same. There were approximately one hundred men in each unit, but the rooms were cleaner in Allach, and we did not have to witness quite so many atrocities as in Auschwitz. If we fell ill, we were treated by Jewish doctors who were also imprisoned at the camp. We had to be able to work at any cost.

Everything was perfectly organized so that all resources were most efficiently utilized. I cheated my way in, and as far as I knew I was the only person there under the age of eighteen. I was the baby in the camp, and that's what they called me. For some strange reason they also called me Churchill. I had learned something about Winston Churchill in school, admired him, and had said so to the others. "There goes Churchill," they would say when they saw me.

Right from the beginning of my stay, I tried to find my mother, but realized quickly that there was not a single woman in the entire area. Yet, I was sometimes lucky in Allach. Possibly because of my age and size, they did not always want me as part of the tougher work teams. I was too skinny and too small, so I often missed the worst assignments.

One day I got lost, and a German, who was also a prisoner, felt sorry for me. He was the driver of a work team being sent to work on the railroad near Karlsfeld, and he took me with him. Once I joined that work detail, I was given a new nickname, one which would follow me until the Liberation. They called me Lazarus. When I asked them why, they explained that according to the Christian Bible, Lazarus was raised from the dead, and here I was a boy who had escaped Auschwitz.

The majority of the German prisoners at Dachau and its sub-camps were cultured Germans, not at all raw and brutal like their countrymen, the SS officers. Seeing Germans as prisoners in the camps put the seed in my brain early on not to lump all Germans together. Even as a boy, I knew this experience was never going to be easily understood with simplistic notions. These particular

Germans had been sent to work camps because they opposed Hitler politically or because they were homosexuals. Many came from good jobs and most were given better work in the camps than us Jews. It looked to us like they lived almost ordinary lives, sometimes even better considering the times.

Each day we were sent in different directions to perform various types of work. I was often sent to nearby Karlsfeld where we worked on the railroad, loading and unloading trains. Some days we were sent to work at the BMW factories that were located nearby. Back then we called them Bayerisch Motoren Werke (Bavarian Motor Factory). They collaborated with the Nazis. Before the war they produced very famous motorcycles, but the factory was changed into a plant that manufactured planes and tanks for the German army.

As time passed that summer, I became very skinny. My bones protruded everywhere. I was terrified that I would faint, and if I did, I did not know what they would do to me. I was truly surprised at just how strong the fear of death remained for me – someone on the outside looking in might think death often preferable to what we were enduring, but deep within me was a strong survival instinct, one focused only on living, no matter what.

Whenever we were sent off to work on the tough jobs, I had no idea if I would drop dead before the day was over, and we worked from early morning to late evening. If I did not have the strength to move fast enough, the SS officers beat me over and over again with their batons. In such moments any of my newfound hope and courage vanished. I did not think I could handle working much longer. My deceit was catching up with me. I sometimes had to carry bags of cement that weighed more than I, dragging them from a truck to a place where the Nazis were constructing something. They kept building factories until the end. I was perpetually scared that the kapo would remove me from the team – then there was no saying what they would do to me. Most kapos were terrible, terrible people.

Each unit had its own kapo. The Nazis appointed them leaders of the barracks. Although they too were prisoners, the kapos were in many ways just as cruel, sometimes even worse, than the SS officers who were in charge of the camps. If one of us escaped, the kapos were held responsible and would be shot. The kapos had greater comforts than most of the prisoners, but they were still scared out of their wits. They decided what we did twenty-four hours a day.

The kapos stayed in separate quarters with only four men to a room. They had proper beds and were given real food. Every Saturday they were even taken to visit the prostitutes in town. Dachau had its very own brothel, and the Nazis were convinced sex would improve the kapos' performance and their morale; however, they still had to wear their traditional striped prison suits during their weekly visits to the brothels.

Among the kapos there was one particularly nasty guard. He made us march, despite the poor shape we were in, like we were soldiers going into battle. We marched through the streets on the way to the BMW factory, and if a German girl passed by, the kapo would really show off. Those who did not march properly were kicked and beaten only to impress some stupid girls.

It is hard to describe what we must have looked like, marching along the streets with the kapo screaming and carrying on, feeling truly powerful. But what exactly was his power? Who did he really control? A bunch of half-dead, Jewish prisoners in a concentration camp.

Fortunately, I had Sandor in my life. We stayed in the same barracks, and he always supported me when things got really tough. At one time we worked in a group that was sent to Munich to clean up after the bombardments. It was hard work, physically and emotionally, as we saw much suffering following those bombings.

The Americans were very exact. Every single day at 12 o'clock they bombed Munich. Then we were sent in, miserable as we were, to clean up and get the city ready for the next attack. Standing in the backs of trucks, we rode into Munich, which was increasingly devastated. Mostly we had to clean up the area around the main train station. This whole situation seemed completely absurd.

When the Germans yelled "bombers," we ran for cover, while at the same time rejoicing at the sight of the American planes – a clear indication that the war was winding down. While covering my head, I looked up happily at the planes and welcomed them in my heart. I loved the Americans for what they were doing. I felt that they were helping us.

However strange it might sound, I sensed that some of the kapos and SS officers at Allach felt sorry for me, and three kapos began treating me humanely. One of them was the most vicious and brutal murderer in the entire camp. Next to Mengele, he was the most dangerous man I have ever met face to face in my life – Christof Ludwig Knoll.

Knoll was a sadist, and there were also rumors that he was homosexual. Some young boys saved their lives by getting involved with those kapos and SS officers who were homosexual, and even though I had no intention of becoming a sexual object, it was very important for Knoll to like me, and he did, initially, because the other kapos also liked me. He, too, called me Lazarus.

A divorced father of two children, Knoll was a communist; he was imprisoned in Dachau as a political prisoner from September 1933 to late April 1945. He eventually became the head kapo at Allach. When not murdering Jews, his additional responsibilities included tending to a medicinal herb garden at the camp.

Initially, all I really knew was that Knoll fancied me. He had red hair, and I can still see his close-set, sunken eyes. They were dangerously mean – the eyes of a psychotic killer. He also had a square, chiseled face and a small mustache. He killed people in a heartbeat. All my friends had seen him kill. He used an axe to behead his victims. Knoll is also infamous for bizarre and sadistic acts in which he forced the prisoners to partake.

One day he sent a group of barefoot prisoners out into the muddy yard to be beaten with sticks. When they came back inside, of course, they tracked the mud into the barracks. Knoll then demanded everyone lick the muddy floors until they were again clean. He beat those who didn't lick fast enough. But Knoll was quite nice to me.

He asked me to give him a manicure. He provided me with a nail file and other accessories, and I taught myself to do it so that he was satisfied. I always hoped that he would ask me again because that was how I won privileges.

A few months earlier I had spent my time playing with my dog in a small Hungarian village. Now I was in Allach, giving a manicure to a murderer. It was insane. Our routine became a heated topic of conversation among my friends, but I felt really privileged. I would do almost anything to survive, and this easy work was safe and not disgusting.

I took advantage of the "friendship" that stemmed from these manicures, and I did get privileges – extra food and shoes that fit. Most importantly, I was not sent out on brutal work details with the other prisoners. I was fast reaching the point where nothing moved me emotionally anymore and nothing shocked me either. I was developing a depraved way of thinking.

In such an unbelievably short time, I had become a desperate being. There was very little difference between myself and a wild animal. I even started to eat the way animals eat. Hunger completely controlled me. This transformation happened so quickly, almost as if I stepped into the cattle car and exited a completely different creature.

Chapter Five: Never Give Up

My youth gave me advantages during my time in Allach. In addition to my favorable treatment from Knoll, an *Oberscharführer,* one of the leaders of the camp, picked me to be his orderly and to assist in his work at the Karlsfeld train station. That meant that when the others had to march out to the toughest work spots, I would go to the train station in Karlsfeld to perform lighter, less demanding tasks. He stayed in a small, furnished barracks near the tracks where he also took his lunch and nap every afternoon. My job was to make sure he was all right and that everything was nice and tidy. I spent most of the day in and around the barracks while the *Oberscharführer* went about his job of brutalizing the prisoners who worked on the tracks.

I now had a good deal of freedom to move around the town, so I began looking for people who would give me food when I begged for it. Sometimes I was successful, but what I was soon to receive that summer was even greater than food. There were two Germans who made everlasting impressions on me during this time. Their kindness eclipsed much of the evil done to me by their countrymen. They also reinforced the idea that I should not put all Germans into the same category.

One such person was Martin Fuss, the train station gatekeeper at Karlsfeld. He noticed me standing across the tracks from him one day and approached me. We struck up a friendship. He would often bring me liverwurst sandwiches and help keep up my spirits with his incredible kindness. Our meetings went on for months.

Many years later I discovered Fuss had a son my age. Perhaps that's why we bonded so closely. But didn't other Germans have also sons my age? What grace allows one person to open his eyes while others remain blind?

Back then I don't think he knew how much his small acts of generosity meant to me, but they helped save my humanity because I was becoming increasingly filled with hatred and hardness. I had become tough, like an animal in many respects – but there was still a human heart underneath that might have been forever poisoned with hatred for all things German – or all things period.

Not long after meeting Martin Fuss, I met a German woman who became like a mother to me; she offered me compassion above and beyond anything I could ever have imagined possible at the time. She became my soul's protector.

Agnes Riesch was a stout woman with a kind face and warm and happy eyes. She was a farmer's wife. One day as she was carrying packages and walking back from the bakery, pushing her bike, I stepped out in front of her, asking if she could spare a small piece of bread. I spoke some German by this time. She looked at me with horror.

As I again reflect upon these events so many years later, I wonder what was so different about her heart that she could not ignore me like so many others had? I was emaciated, bones protruding all over my body. I don't think I had seen my own reflection since leaving my hometown in Hungary, but I must have looked awful.

Full of disbelief, while trying to reconcile the voice and image standing before her, she said: "Little boy, why are you here?" I pointed to my prisoner number.

"Oh, *you* cannot be a political prisoner!"

With just one glance, she seemed to grasp the essence of the crimes being committed in her country, almost as if we had been going through this *together*. Though all the hatred for the Jews was clearly visible to her in my emaciated body, she chose not to look away – and she was determined to counteract that hatred. She then dug into her bag and handed me a large piece of bread – bigger than any slice of bread I had ever seen in a concentration camp. For Germans there was a rationing system, and she gave me half her family's ration of bread, a food coupon, and money so that I could shop at the bakery on my own. Her simple act of kindness and compassion forever changed me.

From then on I always looked for Frau Riesch. I told her my name was Lazarus, and she always addressed me, "My dear son, Lazarus." She actually called me her son. During those summer months when I was in Allach, we met on a weekly basis.

With Agnes Riesch's actual son, Hans, fighting the Russians at the eastern front, her daughter-in-law Fannie preferred to live with her own mother in Munich rather than with Frau Riesch, but at one point Frau Riesch introduced us though I didn't make much of it at the time. Then came the day when the *Oberscharführer* told me he was expecting a visitor and it was imperative that

I keep guard during the visit. No one was to enter his barracks while he hosted his guest.

As the train pulled into Karlsfeld from Munich, I was preparing myself to greet the visitor when suddenly out stepped Frau Riesch's daughter-in-law. Fannie was all dolled up. She was the *Oberscharführer*'s secret caller! Every Thursday thereafter she was on the train from Munich.

The world of romantic love was unchartered territory for me; I had no experiences with women from which I could draw any comparisons. All I knew was that Fannie was beautiful, and she and the *Oberscharführer* had something very special and very different going on inside those barracks as the trains rolled past them hour after hour.

My only job on Thursdays was to prepare the small space for romance, and I would fix up everything as best as I could. I always made sure there was wine on the table. It was made very clear to me that not a single person approach or enter the barracks, under any circumstances, while Fannie had fun on the hard narrow couch the *Oberscharführer* set up for his daily nap.

Of course, the most important person to keep away from his office was his wife. She, too, lived in Munich and was fond of paying her husband unexpected visits now and then. I understood the gravity of my situation, yet it also gave me an upper hand. I knew he was truly worried when he said, "*Lazarus, du musst aufpassen!*" Lazarus, you must pay attention! I was now in a position to exploit the *Oberscharführer*, and even the smallest degree of power or autonomy was an amazing feeling.

Sometimes I saw him reward Fannie with a pair of silk stockings which pleased her greatly. They spent long hours together, and though I did not know exactly what was going on, I sensed that in the middle of this dreadful hell something extraordinary and wonderful was taking place. I was beginning to feel really optimistic that I could survive until the war ended when my time in Dachau abruptly came to an end.

Even though Frau Riesch had given me bread and love, I was in horrible shape, and my health had deteriorated even more by the time they moved us to a new camp several months later. I had no opportunity to say goodbye to her before they herded us into cattle cars for what seemed like yet another endless ride.

Sandor Grosz and I were still together when we arrived at Mühldorf. We were then moved to a nearby sub-camp at Mettenheim. Several thousand prisoners were at this camp, and we all worked on the railroad, mostly unloading concrete. We worked outside, freezing through the winter of 1944-1945, one of the coldest in European history.

This new camp was very brutal. There were no more privileges. I was now slaved at hard labor like everyone else at the town's small railroad station. My weight had dropped to about seventy-five pounds. I again felt as if I were about to break down at any moment. I tried my old methods of encouraging myself, thinking positive thoughts – telling myself I would make it and so forth – but this process was much tougher than before. Each morning we had to march – broken and emaciated, freezing with worn clogs on our bare feet – while our guards beat us with sticks.

The labor was harder than in the other camps, appallingly hard. They were simply trying to destroy us. We were all mere skeletons, and people died all around me – first the guy on the right, then the guy on the left. A man can endure a lot, but then suddenly he can endure no more. I've been told the average life expectancy for a prisoner at Mühldorf during this time period was sixty days.

In our camp there was a young Jewish man from Czechoslovakia named Max Mannheimer. I had first met him back in Allach. Because he spoke fluent German, he was treated a little better than the rest of us. Max was on speaking terms with two German soldiers, so he was able to get quite a bit of information from them. He also learned things by eavesdropping on the guards.

As winter slowly turned to spring, one of the things Max told us was when they sent us marching, things would get really bad. The guards called them death marches because as the Red Army and the Allied forces were approaching, we were soon to be marched on foot, without food or drink, to our deaths. The purpose was to kill us from starvation and exhaustion so that we would not be liberated, thus leaving behind no witnesses to the atrocities.

I was already close to breaking down when the orders came to march from Mettenheim back to the nearby town of Mühldorf. The death march started early in the morning on April 25, 1945. We were a sad, pathetic sight. There was absolutely no food, not even the small rations of bread we usually had. At one point, as we marched through the woods, Max suddenly took off running. He knew too much about what lay ahead. He ran and ran, dashing off as fast as he could into the forest. We all stayed completely quiet, but heard no shots. They did not even attempt to shoot him. Max was so weak that he was easy to catch. When they caught him, they simply put him back on line with the rest of us, marching toward death.

When we arrived back in Mühldorf, we lay down from exhaustion in an open field. The local Germans stared at us. We looked like corpses. The SS had to get us out of there in a hurry in case any of these onlookers started asking too many questions, and we could sense their eagerness to transport us away from Mühldorf as quickly as possible.

That evening, April 25, they put all 3600 of us in cattle cars at the railway station in nearby Ampfing. Around this time, I lost contact with Max, never knowing that he would play a huge role in my life more than sixty-five years later.

We had not had any food for several days, and never did I feel hunger as intensely as then. The train was very long, with perhaps sixty to eighty cars stretching for more than half a mile, so it moved very slowly, and every time the train stopped, I went down on the floor and reached out between the cracks in the floorboards, just able to stick my arm through and pull up some of the grass and weeds that grew between the tracks. I ate that those plants like an animal. Then the others did the same.

After two days, the train came to a complete stop, but we hadn't actually traveled very far. The engine shut down and the doors opened. We were in a small town I would later learn was called Poing. At the platform we saw SS officers tearing off their uniforms, hurriedly dressing in civilian clothes.

"*Alle Frei.*"

"*Alle Frei.*"

"*Alle Frei.*"

The guards were all yelling in unison at the top of their lungs, "*Alle Frei!*" "*Alle Frei!*" Then they took off running.

We stared at each other in shock. We were confused, frightened, and silent. "Free?" We looked at one another. We saw no guards anywhere, and a few of us nervously poked our heads outside the train's doors while repeating that word – "free!"

When the guards didn't return, relief soon spread throughout our group on the train. A few of us agreed to stick together and get hold of some food and water as quickly as possible. We were still dressed in our prison uniforms when we ran, but we had to get away before the Nazis changed their minds or some other terrible thing happened.

We must have been quite a sight, running as fast as we could – which wasn't terribly fast – so skinny that our striped uniforms flapped like sails in the wind. We saw a farm in the distance and headed for it. We were a small group of four, in terrible shape in our stinking uniforms with our bones pressed out against our skin. And that was how we looked when we arrived at the farm kitchen. Once again, I was to encounter a German who defied stereotypes.

As always, I was the youngest in our group, and the wife on the farm took such pity on me that she started to cry. Seating me at the table, she served me a large glass of milk and sliced bread with butter, just like I used to get at my Aunt Ida's farm. I can still see that meal – still smell it and still taste it! I could not believe I was sitting in a peaceful house in the country on a kitchen chair. I remember seeing a crucifix on the wall near the table. In that moment I lost my fear of the Catholic faith, and I thought, *thank God, I am protected.*

With every morsel of bread and milk I was able to swallow, I felt my strength and my happiness coming back. A German woman had again treated me as if I were her son. As filthy as I must have looked, she wasn't afraid to touch me. She sat stroking my hair as I ate as much of that wonderful meal as I could. Though the encounter only lasted a few hours, and I did not learn her name, I thought of this woman every day for the rest of my life.

Later that afternoon, as I was sitting at her table relaxing for the first time in more than a year, three soldiers armed with handguns rushed in. Out of nowhere they stood in the kitchen. My friends were quicker and smarter than I and ran into the bedroom to hide beneath the bed. These soldiers were informed that we had entered the farm, and for them the war was not yet over. They belonged to the Hitler Jugend, Hitler Youth, and came from a training camp nearby. They still believed Germany would win the war and definitely did not intend to surrender.

I made a dash for the door, though I have no idea where I got the strength to run so fast. One of the soldiers pursued me out into the yard. In the middle of my flight, I suddenly came to a fence, an obstacle which I overcame in one quick jump, just like that.

Behind me the German kept yelling, "Stop!"

I kept running into the pasture. Then I heard a snap, like a pop from a firecracker, and all at once I fell, my legs collapsing under me. The bullet entered my neck and exited through my cheek. My jawbone was crushed, and I lay on the ground with blood streaming from a large hole in my face.

Breathless from our sprint, the German huffed and spoke as he caught up to me, "Get – get up."

I stayed on the ground while he bent over me, trying to catch his breath, with his hands on his knees and the gun still in his right hand. He straightened up, "Either you get up or I have to finish you off!"

Though he again pointed the gun at me, he seemed unsure of what to do with it. I don't think he had ever actually been in combat, and the sight of what he had done to me at close range had given him pause, if only for a moment or two.

I found the strength to mumble, "Wait – wait – I'll get up now."

He grabbed me and walked me back to the cattle car waiting on the tracks. On the way to the station, we passed by the most horrific scenes. Other prisoners, who, like us, thought that they would be able to escape, had been caught by the Hitler Jugend and the SS guards and shot while standing up against trees.

At the sight of the dead, I felt lucky to be captured by this inexperienced soldier. At the same time I kept thinking about the boys who had hidden beneath the bed at the farm. I never saw them again. I later learned that some prisoners had been kept safe by local farmers until the war ended a few weeks later. This however was not to be my fate.

Pistol in hand, the teenager, who was only a few years older than I, took me back to the train and pushed me aboard. Walking back to the train station, we passed the bodies of murdered prisoners all over the road. At this time, the prisoners who had survived were forced to gather the bodies of the prisoners who had been wounded and throw them onto the train, yet dead bodies were left scattered about the countryside for anyone to see. The events of this day came to be known as the Massacre at Poing. Fifty-four prisoners were murdered on their way back to the train after the false liberation and more than two hundred were seriously wounded.

The blood stopped running, but large flies ate at my open wound. The pain was unbearable when I tried to swallow or move my jaw in any way. I had never suffered such pain in all my young life, yet I felt fortunate compared to one of my hometown friends, a young man named Roth, whom I recognized when he was also returned to the cattle car after having been shot in the stomach.

Roth still stands out in my mind. He was so religious. Even in the camps he remained Kosher. He cried out in pain all night long and died in the morning as I held him in my arms. He lay dead inside the train for three more days during our interminable trip to nowhere.

After the false liberation and massacre, the long train was now separated into two shorter trains, so it could move faster. The section I was on was eventually headed for Tutzing.

There was so much fear on the train. If the SS guards got angry at a prisoner, they simply opened the door and threw him out. But we soon had another danger. We were subjected to bombardment and strafing by American machine guns, and many more people were killed. Apparently, the Americans thought that we were a German military transport and not miserable prisoners from a concentration camp.

We had a way of shielding ourselves from the large bullets which were flying everywhere – we'd pull bodies of our dead comrades over us and hide beneath what little protection their skinny corpses offered, hoping to block the bullets. Eventually, we got the idea to put dead bodies of prisoners in their uniforms on top of the train, so the American pilots might see we were not German military, but for the rest of the ride, I still crouched down beneath mangled corpses, protecting my gunshot wound with my hand, afraid that I would catch another bullet.

After a three-day journey with intermittent stops along the way, the train finally arrived at Tutzing. When the doors opened, we saw American soldiers everywhere. We had arrived in a liberated area. Now we really were free.

This time it was for real. Yet I was hardly rejoicing when we met the American forces. I could feel nothing but pain. I was so weak I could barely walk. I stumbled around, looking for something to eat, my open wound visible to all. The American soldiers waved and threw chocolate, candy, and cigarettes at us, but I was too weak to get any of it. Every time I thought I had my hands on a piece of chocolate, someone stronger than I took it from under my nose.

All at once, I heard yelling and screaming. It was one of the Hitler Jugend from the train being beaten, almost to death, by former prisoners. But an American lieutenant named Henry Cohen appeared and told them to stop. He said he was also a Jew and sympathized with their rage, but this member of the Hitler Youth had to stand trial and not be killed by Jews in such a bestial manner. He then took the German away from the angry prisoners and drove off with him in a Jeep. In fact, I saw a number of Germans murdered by enraged prisoners seeking revenge for all their suffering. It is amazing how their latent rage was so suddenly and forcefully unleashed, yet I had no interest in such pursuits. I just wanted to live.

While I walked around looking for ways to satisfy my hunger, I found a Hitler Jugend jacket that had been thrown into a ditch. I picked it up and

Picture 7: Prisoners upon liberation at Dachau, May 1945.

examined it carefully. Dusting it off, I then removed the striped prisoner jacket of my uniform and put on this jacket. Instantly, I felt mentally stronger as though I was telling myself, "I am wearing this jacket, but I am not one of them."

Although I was about the right age, I wasn't the least bit worried about being mistaken for a Hitler Jugend. With the last year or so spent in the camps embedded so strikingly into my drawn and mangled face and my emaciated body, there was no chance of that happening. In fact, I became pretty fond of that jacket.

Suddenly, I heard someone shouting my name in Hungarian. It was a friend of my beloved father from my hometown. His surname was Remvny, and he was a doctor. He saw me walking the streets of Tutzing wearing the Hitler Jugend jacket and that huge wound in my face. Referring to the wound in my face, not the jacket, he said, "Are you are crazy, child, walking around like that? You're going to the hospital right now."

He got me admitted to a hospital that was mainly for wounded German soldiers. It turned out that I was infected with typhoid fever from the flies in my wound and was perilously close to death. Typhoid fever is contagious, so I was transferred to yet another hospital in Feldafing – where all the typhoid patients from the area were treated – this area was also the site of a large displaced persons camp.

Feldafing is a beautiful town filled with rich and famous people, and I was in a wonderful hospital – more like a hotel – sleeping in a lovely, clean bed with pillows and blankets. After a few weeks, my jaw though disfigured had healed enough for me to eat. I was fed well, but unfortunately became ill because I stuffed myself with food from the Red Cross. They gave us peanut butter and jelly and candy sent from Switzerland. I was crazy about peanut butter, but had not had any sweets in almost a year, and I did myself no good with the treats.

We all had typhoid fever, and some were delirious. They hallucinated, yelled, and sang, even trying to jump out windows. Everyone wondered how I had survived the shooting. While I was in the hospital, a Jewish doctor told me that something had to be done about my disfigured face. My mouth was now totally crooked because the bones were healing in the wrong way.

Emphatically he told me, "You have to go to another hospital and have an operation."

I jumped up, "No – never!"

There was no way I would undergo an operation. I had suffered enough, and now I wanted to enjoy my freedom, but the truth was that I was terribly afraid of having the operation. As he spoke to me, I was on the brink of tears. Then the doctor said, "The way you look now, not a single girl will want you." I agreed immediately and was then admitted to a military hospital nearby. I was the only Jew among many German soldiers, most of whom had their arms or legs amputated and were suffering terribly. I never spoke to them, but overheard a few of them say to each other, *"Ich bin nicht schuldig,"* I am not guilty. I would turn my face to the wall just trying to imagine they were not there.

A former high-ranking Nazi surgeon who specialized in facial reconstruction operated on me. Once again a German who could just as easily have murdered me was saving me, and once again I again experienced terrible pain. I thought I would lose my mind. The first night they gave me morphine, which was a good thing. The pain disappeared for a few hours, along with all the memories of my suffering. However, I was not allowed any more the next night, though I cried and screamed and begged for relief.

My nurse was a beautiful Catholic nun, and she was exceptionally kind to me because I was the only former concentration camp prisoner in that hospital and still just a boy. She took really good care of me, and so did the German surgeon. In return, I managed to obtain a carton of cigarettes to give him.

I cannot say I enjoyed my newfound freedom because of all the pain I was going through, but I did enjoy washing up each morning. It was luxury to be clean. I had not brushed my teeth in a year, nor had I even seen a piece of soap. Before the Germans got their hands on us, I did not think much about personal hygiene, and it meant nothing in the camps when all we could do was focus on staying alive.

When the immediacy of the fight to stay alive had passed with the end of the war and my liberation, my lost family began to haunt me. During the quiet moments of my recovery in the pleasant hospital room, thoughts of my mother and Judith always returned. I fantasized about them all the time. I wondered where they were. Against all rational thought, I still hoped to see them again.

I felt guilty for having survived. I did not understand why I had not gone with them when the lines diverged at Auschwitz. At least I didn't have to worry about fellow inmates stealing my bread under my mattress. Slowly, I recovered, beginning the long road back.

One day the door to my room opened and Sandor Grosz entered with three other friends from my hometown, Sandor Feldman, Endre Grosz, and Bela Lowy. They didn't waste a moment and teased me because of how I looked. We all laughed. I think it was the first time I had laughed in a whole year. We were all together again.

Picture 8: Leslie Schwartz (left) and Sandor Feldman shortly after the war.

Chapter Six: From the DP Camps to America

The Displaced Person's camp in Feldafing where my friends and I were first placed was formerly a headquarters for SS officers and situated in a beautiful, rural area, yet despite the safety and calm of life there, my dreams were still haunted. I kept having a strange dream about my dog, Friend.

In the dream, she has a typical litter of puppies, eight or nine in all, and my father asks all our neighbors if anyone wants one. We find homes for one or two, but everyone else we ask just shakes his or her head.

I'm just a little boy, six or seven, and as my father and I are walking home, he tells me to get rid of the puppies. He says we cannot keep more than one dog in the house and tells me, "Just take them to the canal and throw them in – that will take care of the problem." I simply listen to him without any sort of emotional response.

There are canals all around the outskirts of town with very cold water running through them. As soon as we get home, I drag all the puppies stuffed in a burlap sack through town down to the canals.

They're yelping and crying as I gently take each little puppy out of the sack and push it into the water. One by one, I watch their tiny bodies disappear as they momentarily struggle to stay afloat, but they're just too small and too weak to make it in the icy water.

As I walk home through town, everyone is smiling and saying "hello" as if nothing unusual has happened. I feel like they're all aware of what I've done, yet no one thinks anything much about it. I know what I've done is horrible, but I don't feel any emotions, like I'm not even human.

In reality, this sort of disposal of unwanted pets was very common where I grew up. Most everyone had dogs and cats. No one ever gave it a second thought. I wake up in the same cold sweat every time.

My father, Imre, had relatives in the United States, and I quickly became obsessed with getting in touch with them. I did not know their names or where they lived. I did not even know if they were still alive, but I did know that my father stashed their letters in the attic of our home in Baktalórántháza. I had to find those letters, even one of them, and hope that it had a return address on the envelope. I told Sandor Grosz about my idea and asked if he would travel back home with me. He was game.

Immediately after the war, transportation was free on all buses and trains, so a number of us traveled together, eager to get back to Hungary. During the last part of the journey, we took a local train, and I recognized two girls from my hometown; they were hearing and speech-impaired sisters whom my friends and I had cruelly mocked when we were young. I thought that they must have hated me and wished me dead.

Seeing me on the train, they recognized me instantly, despite my skeletal body and the Hitler Jugend jacket. Then the unimaginable happened – they got up and hugged me, first one and then the other, holding me tight. And they cried. I felt warmth surge through my heart. This experience truly moved me.

However, seeing my hometown again would otherwise not evoke much positive emotion. My only goal was to find the letters my father had hidden in the attic and to fetch my grandfather's gold watch from our neighbors. I figured I needed it for my survival – to pay for my new life in America.

As soon as we got to town, I walked up the garden path to my childhood home. Another family lived there now. Even our furniture was gone. When I saw other people living in our house, I left. I did not know them, so I calmly walked over to the Pap's place, our neighbors who were kind enough to safekeep Grandfather's watch and the same people to whom I had sent postcards from Auschwitz – one of the strangest anecdotes from my imprisonment. Shortly after we arrived in Auschwitz, we were gathered together, handed pencils and postcards, and ordered to write: "We have arrived and are having a wonderful time. We have been given work. Everything is fine and we are doing well." I addressed these postcards to the Paps, thus helping the Nazis promote their extermination camps.

I'm not sure anyone imagined we would ever return, though none of this mattered to me. I realized quickly, however, how emotionally difficult it was for me to be back in my hometown, not just because people I didn't even know had taken our house, but because of the way everyone else had treated us in the years before we were sent to the concentration camps. The Nazis were one kind of evil, but these Hungarians, formerly our friends and neighbors, somehow seemed even more responsible in my mind.

How could they betray us so completely? What could possibly have been going through their minds to get to that point?

The Paps told me I was welcome to stay with them while I searched for the letters. I asked them to introduce me to the people who had taken our house. It was obvious they knew each other. When I was finally allowed into the attic, I saw that all our belongings had been discarded. They sold whatever valuables we had. Our Persian rugs were gone. I looked for our family photo albums. They were gone, too.

I was feeling both empty and disappointed but also concerned about my life. I knew that there was no future for me in this town. There was no way I would ever live among these people again.

Though I stayed with the Paps for the week I spent in Baktalórántháza, I didn't bring up the watch right away, but I was a little surprised when they didn't mention it either.

The Paps actually had a puppy from my dog Friend. They told me that Friend was gone – when the new family moved into our house, she ran into the woods. I wouldn't have been surprised if they shot her.

Before I left Baktalórántháza for good, thinking the timing was right, I asked Mrs. Pap for my grandfather's gold watch. I told her what my mother had told me: "Remember, if something happens to us, Mrs. Pap has grandfather's watch." Mrs. Pap looked me straight in the eyes and answered: "Your mother took it back before you went away." I knew that was a lie.

On our way out of town, we ran into my friend Bela Lowy's older brother, Frank Lowy. Amazingly, Frank had managed to hide out until after the war, but Sandor and I convinced him He'd have no life if he stayed in Hungary, so he agreed to travel with us back to Germany with the hope of one day going to America.

I left without any further regret or sorrow, but not without trouble. Sandor met two beautiful girls from a wealthy family in a nearby village and he told them that I was fifteen, alone in the world, without any means of support. The morning I intended to leave, Sandor told me in all seriousness that these two Jewish girls wanted to adopt me. They were in their early twenties. Though I was fifteen, I felt like I was fifty. This proposal made me furious.

If I were going to be related to those girls, it would only be by marrying one of them. Besides, at that time I was just beginning to experience my freedom, and being adopted by those girls seemed more like another kind of imprisonment than anything else.

But Sandor insisted, "They're wealthy – their family owns land." I wanted nothing to do with his scheme. Sandor planned for the girls to come and get me at the train station, but I hid until I was able to jump aboard the train to escape. I was relieved, but that only lasted until the train pulled into the next station where I saw the girls standing on the railway platform with Sandor and Frank.

Right on the platform, Sandor was pushing me, saying, "This is your last chance. Go with them!" But my slight frame could not be moved as I dug in my heels, "No – no – I'm not going with them."

He knew I meant it, and I could finally go back to Feldafing in peace. When I think back now, I realize had I taken the girls up on their offer, life would have become very difficult in just a few short years once the Communists took over Hungary in 1949. Their wealth and property were all taken away by the newly formed Communist Government.

So many Hungarians who had participated in the destruction of Hungarian Jews, who willingly sent more than half a million of their former friends and neighbors off to their deaths were soon to be persecuted in similarly horrible ways by the Communists.

When we arrived at the Austrian border, a group of Russian soldiers entered the train asking for our identification papers. These Russians were quite brutal and in no mood to humor any Holocaust survivors, so they ordered us off the train immediately. Frank spoke a bit of Russian and always carried a bottle of vodka in his pocket, and the vodka, better than any passport, came to our rescue, allowing us to move on to Vienna.

The American soldiers were in command in Vienna, and they poured lice-killing powder all over us, just in case we were as infested with vermin as we looked to be. I was still wearing my Hitler Jugend jacket. They too demanded to see our papers, and since we didn't have any, refused us entry into the country. We still managed, somehow, to sneak across the border.

We lived like the homeless boys we were as we tried to make our way back to Feldafing. Though it was against the law and very cold, we slept outside, mostly at train stations. There was no food anywhere, but riding the trains was still free.

Before going back to the DP Camp, I first wanted to go to Munich, to the place where I, dressed in my prison uniform, had been ordered to clean up the mess following the American bombardments. I wanted to feel what it was like to be there as a free man. When we arrived, we were greeted by a horrible sight. In Munich, everything was bombed to pieces. There was devastation everywhere.

Picture 9: Munich town hall, 1945.

The first night in Munich, the three of us slept on the floor in the German Museum; we had no blankets though, and it was simply too cold and damp, so we decided to go back to the displaced persons camp the next day.

We made it to a newly created DP camp in Bavaria called Föhrenwald, just east of Feldafing across beautiful Lake Starnberg. Föhrenwald formerly housed migrant workers and later slave laborers during the war. By 1946, it had become the third largest DP camp in the American sector with over five thousand people living on streets named after states in the US. I lived at 22 New York Street. The complex was enormous and from our perspective very lavish. Inside the camp my emotions began to reassert themselves, albeit quite slowly. But we all had major losses to confront.

I met my cousin's husband, Miklos Grosz, at the camp. He had a halfbrother, Marton Nanasi, who was there with his family, and I spent lots of time with them. I began to feel I was part of this small family, something that was very important to me.

One "family" member was a lovely young girl named Katie. I asked her out for walks, and for the first time in years, I again had romantic feelings for a girl. She was a year older than I was, and she had a boyfriend three years her senior – and he played the accordion. When I started to show her too much attention, she said, "Go away, you little baby." Her rebuff really hurt my feelings, but I swallowed my shame and stuck with Katie and her mother whenever I could.

Frank, Sandor, and I all lived in the same apartment. The camp had the nicest, biggest kitchen, and I loved to go there and get some food whenever I felt hungry. I was where I belonged, among the other survivors of the concentration camps, where things were organized for us. Life began to take on normal qualities that had been absent for so long.

The Americans ran Föhrenwald under UNRRA – United Nations Relief and Rehabilitation Administration. Henry Cohen, the very same US Army Lieutenant I witnessed rescue the Hitler Jugend from the crowd of former prisoners in Tutzing, was the camp's director, and all the officials there did everything they could to help reestablish ties to our Jewish culture and our sense of community. Under these circumstances, people met and love sparked between ragged men and women. The birth rate at Föhrenwald was one of the highest in the world.

As survivors began to dream about what life could be like, I had only one dream – to go to America. But my reality during the winter and spring of 1946 was that my immediate family had been erased. My face had healed, I was in better shape, but I still owned only my Hitler Jugend jacket.

After a short time in the DP Camp, I knew the next thing I needed to do was to visit the kindly Frau Riesch to express my thanks to her for bringing me bread while I was in Dachau. Now it was my turn to help her.

There were no men in her household immediately following the war. Her son was a prisoner of war and her husband was murdered by former prisoners from Dachau. Soon after the Liberation, he was walking home from work one night when survivors went crazy and started doing the same things the Germans had done to them.

I found she had a large, warm home, and when I arrived, she once again greeted me as "dear son, Lazarus." After that first visit, I went to see her every weekend and brought lots of Red Cross rations for her. Whenever she could, she cooked my favorite dishes – liverwurst and German style dumplings. She would do just about anything to make me happy, though I was more often than not the one bringing her food this time as there was very little food to be found right after the war.

On one visit I learned that Frau Riesch's daughter-in-law Fannie had moved back in with her. We recognized each other from her Thursday visits with the *Oberscharführer* at Allach. I was embarrassed, but she was not. She simply said, "Come sleep with me." I was shocked and wondered what this woman wanted with a child like me. Those were strange times.

Restlessness ruled my mind, and I could not sit still for very long. I had to be doing something – anything. I really wanted to travel back to some of the places I had stayed during my imprisonment, to get an update on what had happened and to take advantage of my freedom and the ability to move around as I pleased, yet I kept looking over my shoulder, often imagining an armed SS officer standing behind me.

But even then I was powerfully drawn right back to the places where I had suffered so much pain. Somehow I knew that leaving them behind would be turning my back on my experiences, as if they hadn't happened. In this way I would be turning my back on myself, on what had now made me the person I had become – the survivor who could overcome any obstacle.

I knew if I were ever to be whole again, I needed to bring together, not scatter, the innumerable fragments of my experiences – the people, good and evil, and the memories of my imprisonment – and someday I would actually gather all those people and experiences together in one space in my heart and mind and make peace with them. I did not know, however, that this healing process would take nearly sixty-seven years to come to fruition.

Sometimes I liked to leave the camp to explore the nearby region on my own. This wasn't always the best idea, but I really couldn't help myself. I now had money because I worked in the kosher kitchen and later as a tree cutter at the DP camp. I was paid in Allied money, which was worth a lot compared to the worthless German mark. But just about everywhere I went in post-war Germany, I saw only disaster. The Germans had nothing; they suffered and starved. Many times on my little excursions, I was stopped by American military police who always asked me if I were Jewish and promptly sent me back to the DP camp.

One night I managed to sneak away and find lodging in a small hotel nearby. Unfortunately, they had nothing to eat and only beer at the bar, but I got a room anyway and went to bed for the night.

As I was sleeping, about two o'clock in the morning, two German police officers burst into my room. They came in with their guns drawn. I was terrified. It seemed people had reported someone at the bar wearing a Hitler Jugend jacket. Staring straight into the eyes of a German police officer, my heart almost stopped. Images of Auschwitz and Dachau immediately flashed back into my mind.

He kept staring at me. I was scared out of my wits, but then he said, "I'm looking for SS people, and you don't look like one."

Afterwards this experience gave me an amazing thrill. I believed I really was free. They were not looking for me anymore. More importantly, I no longer had an enemy. I was only sixteen, but handling that encounter gave me real confidence.

Back in Föhrenwald, the British government got permission for me to travel to London. The British were opposed to the idea of establishing an Israeli state but were happy to accept teenagers and offer us a home in the United Kingdom. But I wanted only to go to America.

The Zionist organizations worked on the other side of the fence. They wanted us all to go to Israel. Regarding the politics, I had no strong feelings either way. I certainly wasn't against the idea of an Israeli state, but I also didn't want to live there. The conflict between the two political entities resulted in a fortunate resolution of my situation because in their efforts to sabotage Holocaust survivors' repatriation in England, the Zionists broke into an office at the DP camp and burned all the papers, including mine, so I could not go to London. Then I experienced another miracle in a young life so full of miracles.

It turned out that one of my uncles, my father's brother, Herman Schwartz, lived in Barcelona and had started an extensive investigation to find any survivors of the Schwartz family from Baktalórántháza. He wrote to the mayor of my hometown who responded that Laszlo Schwartz was the only survivor and was living in a DP camp in Feldafing, Germany. I had left Feldafing by then, so it took a while for the correspondence finally to find its way to me at Föhrenwald.

Meanwhile, my uncle Herman in Spain forwarded the message to his brother, Milton (formerly Miklos) Schwartz in Los Angeles, and once Milton learned of my survival and my whereabouts, he contacted me immediately. He wrote: "Come! We are waiting for you – your entire family in America!"

That letter changed everything, but I almost did not get it. It was confiscated by a bunch of Zionist boys who went around the camp and stole the letters we received from relatives around the world. The day my uncle's letter arrived at the DP camp, the boys stole an entire bag of mail. Luckily, this time they were caught by the military police. The mail was retrieved and distributed. I was in my room, and it was truly a surreal experience when the letter was handed to me. I cannot describe the feeling inside me when I read these words:

We have a photograph of you as a baby.

In the quiet of my room, I kept repeating over and over: "I have cousins in California. I have an uncle who found me and wants me to join his family. He owns a butcher shop in Los Angeles. They have a picture of me as a baby!"

Picture 10: Leslie Schwartz at seven months of age

That picture was better than a passport or citizenship or even money because it meant I was indeed a human being – not a number or a political prisoner.

I had actually been born into a family and had an identity separate and distinct from the one developed during the war and my imprisonment. That picture was proof. I was someone's child once. I was loved.

The social workers and officials were most keen to send children out of the camp. Still, a lot of orphans had to stay for years because they had nowhere to go. Föhrenwald remained open until the last survivors left in 1957, but I was soon going to be on a boat headed for America, only because my family had found me and offered me a home. After reading the letter over and over again, I ran to the UNRRA office and proudly showed it to them. "Look," I cried, "I have an uncle! I have an uncle in America!"

Though I hadn't previously met my family in the United States, somewhere, far away, there were people with the same blood as mine running through their veins, and they were waiting for me to join them. I firmly believed I could only start a new life in America.

I traveled with another Hungarian, Laszlo Niederman. He was five years older than I was and sensationally handsome, at least he thought so. We boarded the train from Munich to Bremen. It was almost like a military transport. I was still wearing my Hitler Jugend jacket; I simply did not want to get rid of it, and there was no place to buy clothes anyway.

On the train we met a beautiful girl who fell for my handsome Hungarian friend. She was on her way back to her family in America. She had only gone to see her grandparents in Germany for a short visit. The war broke out and she could not get out of the country. She was very sophisticated, and my friend fell completely in love with her, too.

However, when we boarded the *SS Marina Perch* in Bremerhaven, she met an American soldier who was returning home after serving in Germany, and from that moment on paid no more attention to my friend. While he suffered from seeing them together on the ship, I suffered from the torment of seasickness.

I was seasick during the entire journey, and the only food available was salted herring, but none of that mattered when the Statue of Liberty appeared on the horizon along with the incredible New York skyline. I was in America at last.

Social workers greeted us as we disembarked on July 27, 1946, and each took responsibility for six children. I spent my first week in America in an awful orphanage in the Bronx. I quickly learned I also had relatives on the East Coast, and when they found out my location, a cousin of mine, Jack Schwartz, showed up to pick me up. Jack was my father's nephew and a recent combat veteran. I thought, *he drives his own car? I must have very wealthy relatives!*

My family in New York all lived in Brooklyn. When I first saw my Aunt Ethel Weinberger, I instantly recognized her. I will never forget that meeting. She had the same face as my Aunt Ida in Hungary, and both of them looked exactly like my grandfather. It was an amazing moment. I longed to have a family with whom I could identify and knew me in return, and here they were.

My eyes were glued to her lips when she spoke about my father. I was curious about every little detail she could tell me about him, but she couldn't remember much since she came to the United States in 1900. I kept pressing her for more details, but she told me, "wait – just wait until you are as old as I am – we'll see what *you* remember."

I just really needed someone to connect me to my family again, but I didn't spend much time with my relatives in Brooklyn. I was off to see my family in California. A social worker with the American Jewish Committee took me by train to Los Angeles, the trip sponsored by my uncle.

Milton Schwartz brought his family, including five children, from Hungary to the United States in 1939. He opened a butcher shop in Los Angeles though he was rather worldly and sophisticated for a butcher. In fact, he had traveled all over Europe before settling down in Los Angeles.

He was Orthodox observant and very intent on bringing me back to the practice of my faith. This road would prove a difficult path for me to walk as my time in the camps had the peculiar effect of challenging any beliefs I had previously held in a supreme being. I had a mighty struggle reconciling images of babies being thrown into the gas chambers in Auschwitz with any concept of God I could envision.

Nevertheless, my Uncle Milton made a grand impression on me when he picked me up from the train station that Friday afternoon. A handsome and self-confident man, Uncle Milton's first words to me were, "Your father lent me money which I never paid back."

The first time in many years the complete range of emotions again flooded my heart and soul was on that very first Friday evening I spent in my uncle's home. Friday evenings are holy for the Jewish people, and as we celebrated the Shabbat, I began to remember similar days spent with my family in Hungary.

Though I was sixteen years of age, that September I was sent to an elementary school in Los Angeles. The neighborhood had mostly Jewish and Mexican people living there. I didn't speak English or Spanish, so I had no way of communicating with anyone, but I could play soccer and impressed my Mexican classmates with my skills. Soccer went a long way toward endearing me to them. After a while they fought to see who could get me on their team.

As far as I knew I was the only Holocaust survivor in that school system, and when I think back, there were so many people who went out of their way to help me at this most vulnerable and shaky time in my life.

Picture 11: Leslie in Los Angeles, 1946.

My elementary school teacher's name was Lea Astash. She was Jewish, originally from the Ukraine, and she spoke Yiddish, a language I had learned from the Polish people I met in the camps. Lea was a beautiful woman in her early fifties, and she lived with her sister in Beverly Hills. Her sister had married a movie producer.

One weekend Lea invited me to her home. My Uncle, being Orthodox, didn't quite approve of my staying over there; I'm not sure what he thought was going to happen, but spending those two days in Beverly Hills after leaving the hell of the camps and the war only a short time before was a life-altering experience for me.

Lea and her sister lived in complete luxury with a beautiful room that seemed just for me. The entire weekend was simply miraculous. Spending time with Lea did wonders for my wounded psyche, and I will be forever grateful for the kindness and compassion she showed me. She gave me a window to see into a world I could never have imagined – that such beauty and luxury even existed and that someone was willing to share it with me, acting as if I deserved to feel happy and comfortable was a revelation.

I also loved spending time with my cousins; they spoke Hungarian, making me feel at ease. We spent our free time in drug stores in Los Angeles; back then there were soda fountains with milk shakes and ice-cream sodas in every drug store and not many other places a teenager would rather be, except maybe the movies. My Uncle Milton also loved the cinema. He was always taking everyone to the movies, and there was one particular film he insisted I see – *The Jazz Singer* with Al Jolson – the first movie I ever saw in the United States.

I sat spellbound in a beautiful theater in Los Angeles, watching a movie about a Cantor's son, Jackie Rabinowitz, who struggles with his father's dream for Jackie to become a Cantor, like many generations of males in his family before him, against the boy's desire to become a pop singer. This theme seemed eerily relevant to my actual situation, especially sitting there with my Orthodox Uncle.

I watched an early scene in the film in which a young Jackie gets beaten by his very stern father for singing Jazz on the night of the Yom Kippur services. Jackie then runs away; he is about the same age I was when I was sent to Auschwitz, when I lost my family, and as his weeping mother says, "Our boy has gone and he is never coming back," I broke down in tears. All Jackie takes with him when he leaves home is a picture of his mother.

Many years later as Jackie's father is dying, Jackie must choose between his emerging career as a Broadway singer (the play he is set to star in opens on the same night as Yom Kippur) and to honor his dying father's wish that he sing Kol Nidre at the Yom Kippur services in his father's place. Somehow Jackie does sing in the synagogue and is still able to keep his Broadway career as his father's spirit watches over him.

I was simply amazed that the first American talkie focused on such a theme and plot, and seeing this movie gave me the feeling that I was protected in the United States. Instead of being denigrated and made the object of scorn and ridicule, my Jewish heritage was respectfully and seriously displayed on a huge screen, for everyone to see.

A few months later, while I was taking a shower, my uncle knocked on the bathroom door and said, "There is a letter for you." It was from Sandor Grosz. He had arrived in America. He was living with his aunt in New Brunswick, New Jersey. That's when I knew I had to move back East.

Once I arrived in New York, Sandor and I quickly recaptured the closeness we had shared through the camps, and we were practically inseparable for a long time. One weekend he would come to Brooklyn where I lived, and another weekend I would go to New Brunswick to stay with him. He got a job as a tailor for a clothing store and was soon able to buy a car. We traveled all over the eastern United States and Canada, often visiting his brother Endre in Montreal.

Picture 12: Their early days in the United States – Leslie Schwartz with Sandor Grosz (right).

My friendship with Sandor was so critically important to me at that time because Sandor and I had lived through the same experiences during the war. We shared a bond few can understand. Besides, a survivor of the Holocaust can never get enough love, and love is what heals, especially if the sickness originated from hatred.

Chapter Seven: Closure and Connection

Getting to know my east coast family was equally wonderful. I lived with my Aunt Ethel Weinberger at 579 St. John's Place in Brooklyn, New York. I quickly developed a close relationship with her daughter-in-law, Helen Weinberger, formerly Helen Long. She had married Ethel's son, Arthur Weinberger. Helen's father, Dr. Jacob Long, came from a long line of German Jews. In his medical practice, long before the days of insurance or government safety nets, Dr. Long had a well-earned reputation for treating the needy at no cost. He was elderly when I first met him and suffering from dementia. I have the oddest memory of eating dinner with their family and feeding Dr. Long strawberry jam as if he were a small child.

At the time I still spoke little English, and those early days and months in America were always a bit strange. I even think I took all my newfound blessings for granted because as a survivor, I felt I had good things coming to me. Maybe my heart was just so ready to soak up all the love. In spite of any struggles or difficulties I faced adjusting to my new life in America, I always felt very optimistic, like each new day was an opportunity for something different and exciting.

My cousin Helen came to mean everything to me. I considered her like yet another mother. She truly cared about me. She also taught me to love America and the rules for being an American from her point of view. The main idea she instilled in me was the concept that Americans were different than the rest of the world because of their compassion. There was nothing more important to Helen than charity. As a good citizen of the United States, it would also be my responsibility to care for those less fortunate – to look out for those who couldn't help themselves. Even with all the trials I had just recently endured in the camps, she taught me not to focus solely on my own problems. She lived these values every day.

When Helen first met me, she barely associated with her Jewish heritage, but my experiences inspired something in her to reconnect with it. She actually started going to the synagogue on Friday and Saturday again.

Helen had three children, Harold, Judith, and Laura. I was always a novelty among her children, and they constantly wanted to expose me to everything "American." Harold was a few years younger than I, and he got me hooked on baseball. Harold took me to Ebbets Field to see the Brooklyn Dodgers during their glory days from 1947 through 1957 – we saw all the great stars like Duke Snider, Roy Campanella, Gil Hodges, and, of course, Jackie Robinson. When the Dodgers left New York for California, I became a Red Sox fan because I could not stand the Yankees who beat the Dodgers in the World Series five times during those ten years. Helen and Arthur were both teachers in the New York City school system, and they had a resort home upstate near the Massachusetts border in a little town called Copake, New York. Copake is located in a beautiful, rural area, and spending time there reminded me of my childhood in Hungary. There was a community of teachers from the city who had second homes in the area, and we all had wonderful times together.

Helen's husband Arthur taught music at Prospect Heights High, formerly Girls Commercial High, and she taught business at Jefferson High in Brooklyn, which is also where I went to school.

Jefferson High was the only New York City high school that taught English to foreigners; the school offered programs for refugee children with special orientation classes to familiarize them with American customs, and the administrators even assigned a faculty advisor to each foreign student in order to facilitate his or her transition process. I thought all the Jewish immigrants in the city must have gone there. They even had a Hebrew Department run by Dr. Edward Horowitz – the only one of its kind in a public high school anywhere. There were many Holocaust survivors in that school, but I didn't talk much about my experiences in those days, and neither did anyone else. Jefferson High had a very solid academic reputation, and many of those students pursued higher education and advanced degrees. But college wasn't in my future.

I started working even before I graduated high school. I worked as a delivery boy for a printing company on Varick Street in Manhattan called Hinkhouse Printing. They were a very creative printing company, and it was there that I first developed my love for the printing business. I worked with mostly African-Americans in the delivery service.

My work consisted of running around the city delivering printing jobs in the afternoons after school, late nights, and on weekends, too. On one brutally cold day during the winter of 1947, one of the black kids said, "It's too cold for us. Send the Jew out." His comment really hurt me, and this experience was my first awareness of any sort of racial problems or anti Semitism in the United States. Being so new to the country, I didn't in any way understand the racial situation in America.

Where I grew up in Hungary, I had never even seen a black man. My first experience with African-Americans was when I was in the DP camp in Feldafing. The black soldiers drove the motor pools, and they brought us food. They were always very cordial and treated us wonderfully. When I came to the US and saw how blacks were treated as second class citizens, even after having served in the war, I just could not comprehend any of this, especially the slight from my black co-worker.

The day I graduated from Jefferson High, Helen's husband, Arthur, came into my room and sat down to have a talk with me. He told me that my Aunt Ethel was getting old, and since Helen's father, Dr. Long, was suffering from dementia, he required a great deal of time and attention; in short, my presence in their home was putting added stress on an already fragile order. They also had three children of their own living there. He said I needed to find another place to live. He left me alone in my room to think things over.

I loved my Aunt and cousins so much, and I enjoyed having a family again, so this request hit me pretty hard. I remember crying like a baby as I went through my small room in their brownstone and packed up my things, saying to myself, "Here I go again – no one wants me."

I used to give Aunt Ethel money from my pay, and I thought I was helping her out, but I suppose Arthur was right in a way. As a teenager, always coming and going at strange hours, any noise I made was heard by everyone. I left quickly though I felt abandoned once again. I rented a room only a few blocks away so I could stay close to everyone.

After working for a few years, I tried to enlist in the United States Army, but they wouldn't take me based on my medical history. Then, in 1953, I got the shock of my life.

I was coming home from work in Manhattan on the subway. I had another job in the printing business by then and lived in Boro Park, Brooklyn. I overheard two women speaking Hungarian, so I approached them. They asked me my name.

"Leslie Schwartz," I said.

They both replied in unison, "We were with your mother and sister in the camps."

I sat speechless, trying to maintain my composure. They didn't know the entire story, but they told me my mother and sister Judith had actually survived the camps. They had been alive until just five days before the Liberation. My half-sister Eva had been gassed upon arrival in Auschwitz, but the women who had been with my mother and Judith told me what happened to them – something about being blown up on a ship in the Baltic Sea. These two women were also supposed to be on that ship, but it was too crowded, so they never made it on board.

I later discovered that on May 3, 1945, five days before the war ended in Europe, the British, on orders from Sir Arthur Cunningham of the Royal Air Force, bombed four ships in the Baltic Sea that were carrying 10,000 concentration camps survivors. My mother and sister must have been aboard one of them. The people aboard came from many different camps including Stutthof, Mittelbau-Dora, Neuengamme, and others. During the war crimes trials, the Nazis said they were sending the ships to Sweden, but others testified that all the prisoners on the ships were going to be murdered on Himmler's orders. The Germans never got the chance to kill those Jews because the British, thinking the ships were only carrying escaping SS officers, did it for them.

In a tragic military mistake, which turned out to be one of the biggest maritime losses of life in history, they were sunk by the Typhoons of 83 Group of the 2nd Tactical Air Force. Some historians say when the British commanders became aware that the deceased passengers were concentration camp survivors, they withheld the information from their pilots – who used sixty pound rockets, bombs, and twenty millimeter cannons to do the job. Even as would be survivors were thrown overboard with the attacks, SS officers who had been onboard and secured lifejackets were shooting the victims in the water as they tried to reach lifeboats. The few emaciated prisoners who managed to swim through the frigid waters of the Baltic Sea to shore were gunned down by Nazis waiting on the beach. The ships were the *Cap Arcona*, the *SS Deutschland*, the *Thielbek*, and a shuttle called the *Athen*. Skeletal remains of those murdered washed ashore for almost thirty years afterwards.

There is no way I can describe how this revelation affected me. I still have never completely come to terms with the knowledge of how my mother and sister were killed. I know, however, that my intuition – that special feeling that kept nagging at me – never let me rest. Even as I was moved from camp to camp as the war was winding down, I always felt in my gut they were still alive. I never stopped believing that somehow we might all be reunited.

I grieved silently and painfully for a long while, but my life eventually had to be focused back on the affairs of the living and making a decent life in America. There was simply nothing else I could do about my mother. There is a point we must all surrender to fate – a time in life when any further struggle only prolongs suffering. I've come to believe that the measure of someone is not what one achieves but what one overcomes. I was determined to get on with my life.

I eventually became the owner of a successful printing company in New York City. I am amazed at the network of associates and friendships I was able to develop, some with whom I still keep in contact, and at how many of them were powerful influences in American politics and culture. Leona Helmsley, the infamous Hotel owner and real estate entrepreneur nicknamed "The Queen of Mean" was among my best clients. I was also related to a very famous American though I didn't meet him for many years.

My cousin on my father's side, the actor Tony Curtis, was born Bernard Schwartz to Hungarian immigrant parents, Helen Klein and Emanuel Schwartz. His parents came to the United States after World War I. Tony served honorably in the US Navy and was wounded in the Pacific during World War II. He was just starting his famed acting career in Los Angeles when I knew of him. My uncle Milton Schwartz took me every Friday and Saturday to the synagogue when I was in California, and I sometimes met Tony Curtis' father there.

I always asked him, "When can I see your son?"

There was always an excuse, "Well, you know, he's a very busy guy – perhaps sometime." In fairness to him, he probably was very busy making a name for himself – he signed his first acting contract in 1948.

Everyone loved Curtis for his role in *Some Like It Hot* (1959), in which he starred with Marilyn Monroe and Jack Lemmon, ranked by many critics as the number one American comedy of all time. In fact, in a career lasting more than fifty years, he acted in well over one-hundred films and was considered one of the last great stars of Hollywood's golden age. Not many people know he was also a great visual artist. He even wrote novels and other books.

Later in life when he had personal problems and his career had faded, he went back to Hungary. He wanted to know exactly where his father came from.

Curtis' father was a tailor in New York City, and Tony established a foundation in his name – The Emanuel Foundation for Hungarian Culture, headquartered in Manhattan. By this time, the early 1980s, my printing company was big, and the president of the foundation called me and told me, "Your cousin is here in New York at the Hyatt Hotel; he would like to see you." I thought, *Now he wants to see me – after he is all finished with his acting?*

I phoned him. With no more managers or secretaries, he picked up the phone himself. The first thing I said to him was, "When I was a kid, you wouldn't see me!"

We later sat down and talked, and two very good things came out of our meeting. Through my business contacts, we were able to raise about ten million dollars for his foundation, with one such fundraising venture a $500 a plate dinner. It seemed every wealthy older woman in New York who had ever been enamored of Tony Curtis showed up to have her hand kissed by Curtis himself. All his old charm and charisma came out once again that night, and for a few hours he was every bit as glamorous and electric as he had ever been in so many of his classic films.

One of the Emanuel Foundation's major projects was to restore the magnificent Dohany Synagogue in Budapest. He also restored many of the Jewish cemeteries in Hungary. In a small way, I was contributing to Curtis' desire to return Jewish culture and tradition to its rightful place in modern Hungarian society and to begin healing the deep and tragic wounds Jews endured there. I felt great about that.

Additionally, I first met Tony's daughter Kelly during that time, and so many years later the real miracle concerning my ties to Tony Curtis is my ongoing relationship with all his daughters: Kelly, Allegra, Alexandra, and Jamie Lee. They have become like a second family to me.

Kelly is Tony's eldest daughter from his marriage to Janet Leigh, and she recently spoke about our reunion just this year: "He and I found a connection almost immediately. I think we both wanted it. My father died a year ago. We just celebrated his yahrzeit (one-year anniversary of a death), and at the end of that first year, suddenly Leslie comes into the picture."

I know their grandparents played a very important part in the girls' lives when they were young; Kelly even told me of a Hungarian lullaby they sang to her that Kelly is still able to recite. But as many of the older members of the Curtis family have passed away, Kelly now considers me something of a wisdom keeper.

When I lost my father as a young boy and later my entire immediate family at Auschwitz, perhaps the greatest loss was the connection to my family history – the stories of my ancestry gone forever. I think Kelly felt the same way with her father's passing until we came back into each other's lives.

A reporter in Florida wrote a story about us. In it Kelly remarked, "As kids we didn't hear about these relatives. We didn't hear the stories about the Holocaust. And here was Leslie, living with these horrors, all of his life." I was moved to tears as I read Kelly's words in *The Palm Beach Post*: "Leslie is a mitzvah. He's a blessing from my father. It's like a life force that my father sent me, and I don't want to miss the gift."[3]

---

[3] O'Connor, Lona. "Holocaust Survivor from West Boynton Bonds with His Cousins, the Daughters of Tony Curtis." *West Palm Beach News – Breaking News, Local Headlines & Weather The Palm Beach Post*. 19 Feb. 2012.

Chapter Eight: Finding Wholeness

I've gone back to Germany for many summers beginning in the 1970s. I even maintain a small residence there. My relationships with those who helped me were too important to let slip away. For more than three decades, I kept up my correspondence with Agnes Riesch. I always made certain that my American family sent her food right after the war, when there was little food to be found. She struggled terribly in those years.

I last visited her in 1972 with a reporter from the German tabloid newspaper *Bild Zeitung*. News of our reunion even traveled back to New York. A photograph of me handing Agnes Riesch a huge loaf of bread was featured in some of the New York newspapers.

Over the years I also stayed in touch with Martin Fuss, the Karlsfeld station gatekeeper who gave me sandwiches and offered me hope for humanity while I was at Allach. When he became very ill, I was glad I was able to send him some medication from the United States that was unavailable in Germany at the time. When Fuss died, I developed a relationship with his son, Martin Fuss Jr., and I remained in close contact with him until his passing in February 2012.

In April 2010, accompanied by my second wife, Annette, I again went back to Germany just as I have for many years. But that summer was unlike any of the previous years because everything began to change for me. After sixty-five years, I was warmly received as an honored guest in Germany – the country responsible for the murder of my family and all my torment. I was able to tell my story to hundreds of people there as a living testimony of former times, and suddenly they wanted to listen.

That summer we heard that in the community of Poing, near where I was shot in the farmer's field during the false liberation, government officials were going to establish a memorial to the Jews killed on the death train, and there was one person from that time who never left my mind. For all those years,

Picture 13: Agnes Riesch and Leslie, 1972.

I wondered about the farmer woman who gave me that wonderful milk and bread, but I had never been able to find out her identity.

Once I arrived, I contacted Poing's mayor, Albert Hingerl; he told me that Heinrich (Henry) Mayer, the local history teacher and his students had researched and collected records of all the incidents in the town before the Americans arrived. Mayer worked with Heinrich Zintl, head of the concentration camp memorial at Dachau, who found my name on the prisoners' list, neatly typed, along with all my fellow sufferers.

Seeing my name on that list seemed more like revisiting a past lifetime, yet I became filled with curiosity wanting to learn about any and all details of the experience that had earlier been denied me. Though I had been there many years before, Zintl again invited me to visit the Dachau memorial on a Thursday in July 2010. This was a very moving experience for me and Annette.

That day I was interviewed for the archives. This was the first time I had ever spoken in Germany about my imprisonment. Previously, in 2007, when the Danish version of my story, *Surviving Hell*, was released, I spoke briefly of

Picture 14: Leslie and Annette.

my experiences in Copenhagen at two public events. But during this two-hour interview at Dachau, I revisited my entire life until I broke down and had to stop. When I walked out, there were young people who had come from all over the world and were eager to chat with survivors, but I was in such bad shape that I couldn't talk to them.

The following day I was received very cordially by Dr. Stephan Wanner, the mayor of Tutzing. Dr. Wanner would come to play a huge role in my healing process over the next few years. On this trip, I also visited the former military hospital in Feldafing where the German surgeon had restored my jaw and fixed my face. The Hotel Empress Elisabeth, a luxury hotel with an adjoining golf course is now housed in that magnificent building.

Later that week I spent Sunday in Poing with Mayor Hingerl who gave me all of his time and attention. I was finally able to learn the name of the wonderful woman who burst into tears when she saw me, sat me down at her table, and fed me the delicious bread and butter with that fresh and foamy glass of milk.

100.Wechsler Lajos	Sch-Jude	71212	11.10.26	Schneiderlehrling
101.Zabak Abraham	"	71219	19. 5.24	Schneider
102.Weiss Emanuel	"	71220	29. 1.27	Feldarbeiter
103.Weiss Jozsef	"	71223	7.12107	Magaeineur
104.Weisz Marton	"	71226	20.12.95	Feldarbeiter
105.Weisz Sandor	"	71228	24. 9.28	Arbeiter
106.Weinberger Miklos	"	71233	15. 9.05	"andwirt
107.Weinberger Salamon	"	71234	31. 5.29	Schüler
108.Czitrom Jakob	"	71243	10.12.98	Kaufmann
109.Czitrom "ajos	"	71244	7. 3.24	Arbeiter
110.Roth Hermann	"	71250	11. 2.97	Beamter
111.Schneck Salamon	"	71251	12. 9.39	Arbeiter
112.Schwarz Laszlo	"	71253	12. 1.30	Student
113.Salamon Nandor	"	71255	15. 9.27	Schüler
114.Smilovits Mixik	"	71257	21. 9.99	Feldarbeiter
115.Bachner Zsigmond	"	79056	24. 3.97	Verwalter
116.Barta Gyula	"	79045	27.12.01	Landwirt
117.Baum Zsigmond	"	79050	10.12189	Landarbeiter
118.Brück Jozsef	"	79093	2. 4.28	Arbeiter
119.Brück Endre	"	79102	11. 2.06	Arbeiter
120.Brust Jozsef	"	79104	9. 5.26	Lehrling
121.Deutsch Laszlo	"	79127	21. 7.01	Spediteur
122.Fischer Sandor	"	79183	21. 6.92	Koch
123.Frankel Jenö	"	79198	24. 8.98	Landarbeiter
124.Freund Arthur	"	79201	12. 3.96	Landwirt
125.Fried Bessedek	"	79204	9. 5.94	Arbeiter
126.Friedmann Mor	"	79215	14. 8.87	Schneider
127.Gans Miklos	"	79225	3. 1.01	Arbeiter
128.Glass Sandir	"	79233	2.11.07	Bäcker
129.Goldstein Gyula	"	79250	1. 8.06	Buchdrucker
130.Grosz Karly	"	79267	28.12.92	Arbeiter
131.Gubi Salamon	"	79266	30. 6.91	Fleischer
132.Harmexschmied Miksa	"	79292	23. 8.96	Landwirt
133.Hoksch Armand	"	79298	7. 3.90	Buchdrucker
134.Hollösünssö Jozsef	"	79323	15. 9.87	Buchhalter
135.Horn Bela	"	79325	3.11.97	Textilarbeiter
135.Kalisch Robert	"	79333	4. 5.91	Arbeiter
137.Kalemen Jenö	"	79350	6. 7.93	Kaufmann
138.Kessler Jenö	"	79360	4. 9.26	Fleischer
139.Klein Zoltan	"	79377	15.10.97	Arbeiter
140.Kraus Emil	"	79422	4. 8.98	Kaufmann
141.Melzer Gustav	"	79478	28. 4.97	Beamter
142.Müller Viktor	"	79495	13. 9.95	Kaufmann
143.Neuhaus Sandor	"	79517	24. 4.27	Rohrflechter
144.Neuhaus Sandor	"	79518	26. 2.93	Arbeiter
145.Neuhauser Benö	"	79521	27.10.97	Kaufmann
146.Popik Vilmos	"	79543	12. 5.01	Chauffeur
147.Pressburger Ignac	"	79553	16. 6.99	Arbeiter
148.Raab Jenö	"	79556	15. 6.92	Kaufmann
149.Renyj Gyula	"	79562	18. 7.93	Beamter
150.Heismann Alaios	"	79563	12. 8.02	Fahr.Monteur

Picture 15: Laszlo Schwarc-Number 112 on the Dachau prisoners' list.

Picture 16: Leslie revisits Dachau, 1972

A journalist named Otto Hartl who accompanied me during my trip had written a series of articles in the local newspapers; one of them reached a descendent of the fine woman. Her name was Barbara Huber; she wasn't young when I landed on her doorstep in 1945 and had long since died, but I was able to have an extensive talk with her daughter, Marianne Meier. As we drank coffee and ate cake, she showed me pictures of her mother and the farmhouse that never left my mind. Though Marianne was a young child at that time, she also remembered what happened on that terrible day, April 27, 1945.

The next day I accompanied Henry Mayer and spoke to more than two-hundred students in his history course at the Franz-Marc Gymnasium school in Markt Schwaben. Of course, this was the first time I had ever spoken to German students and only the second time since being interviewed for the archives at Dachau that I ever spoke publicly in Germany about the Holocaust. Surprisingly, I wasn't at all nervous. The students were very interested in what I had to say and listened intently. I had a good feeling the entire afternoon.

Even when I was still in the camps, I always knew one day I would be-

Picture 17: Leslie revisits Dachau almost 40 years later. Photo by Siri Maria

ar witness, and by talking to those young people in a group setting, where I could see their responses to my story, something wonderful and completely unexpected happened to me that afternoon. This one talk began a renaissance in my life – all because of the genuine love and affection I received from those students.

There is no other way I can describe the experience except to say the most love I have ever felt has come from meeting with German secondary students. When I visit a class, almost as soon as I'm leaving, I'm anxiously awaiting the next visit. I now live for these opportunities, and wherever I go, I receive the same genuine affection. The students are always shocked that the atrocities I endured happened right in their own backyards. They feel honored to have me speak to them, to share my story and my pain, and I'm always willing to answer any and all questions they have.

Their love has healed me in a profound way, and I have been truly nourished by this process. To receive this energy and emotion in the shadow of places where I once received torment is sometimes still unimaginable and always amazing. The descendents of the enemy that would have destroyed me without a second thought have become my source of hope and sustenance. It took three generations for this change to become reality, but it has happened.

Though I didn't always realize it at the time, my going back, again and again, to revisit my experiences was driven by a mysterious force within me. Right from the earliest days after the war ended, I was obsessed with revisiting everything and everyone, and this compulsion never let me rest. The process was often like trying to put together a jigsaw puzzle with missing pieces; frustrated though I was at times, I had to keep searching to bring the lost picture in the puzzle to life.

After speaking with those students, I realized what was missing. Their compassion and willingness to embrace my suffering has made me whole because I'm no longer alone on my journey. They want to go with me, to get to that place of peace and reconciliation together.

My dedication to Germany involves my desire to go back and to give back – to thank the Germans who went out of their way to save my life and my humanity during the darkest times of my imprisonment. I always sought opportunities to return that love, to help the people who helped me, and now I can give something back to their descendents that is truly priceless – my story.

Another wonderful and completely unexpected event during the summer of 2010 was reuniting with Max Mannheimer. I had merely mentioned his name to someone that summer, and I was immediately put in touch with him. He is now very well-known in Germany for giving lectures on his experiences in the concentration camps, the Third Reich, and the Nazi regime. He has spoken to tens of thousands of German students and has said of himself, "I'm here talking as a witness of that period of time, not as accusant or a judge."

Max and I were together at the end of the war. I first met him in Allach, and we stayed close, even as we were moved to Mühldorf. He was the one who by speaking fluent German got us all the information from the SS guards. We remained together on the so-called Mühldorf death train, survived the Massacre at Poing, eventually to be liberated together at Tutzing. I hadn't seen him for sixty-five years.

In spite of his age, he is now past 90, he works tirelessly to enlighten and inform people – to prevent them from forgetting the Holocaust and for improving humanity and democracy. A documentary film called *The White Raven* –

Max Mannheimer (2009) details his amazing work. Max has also been awarded many international honors, including the *Knight of the French Legion.*

He has certainly become a role model for me. So much of my transformation has come about from reconnecting with Max and following his lead. I'm always so impressed and inspired by his busy schedule of speaking engagements at schools and his amazing energy.

One late summer day, on the Sabbath, I greeted Max at his home in Haar, east of Munich. A lovely nun named Sister Elijah regularly looks in on Max, and she was very moved by seeing us together again.

He greeted me at his home by blowing the Shofar, as if calling for the resurrection of those who have passed. The ram's horn announces the New Year in the Jewish community and also the call to do penance. At the same time, it heralds the liberation of the Jewish people.

I asked him, "Max, where did you get this?"

He told me, "This was left in Auschwitz, in Birchanau, on the train. It was recovered by a Polish Christian lady."

That afternoon was one of the great experiences of my life because being reunited with Max further reinforced and solidified my sense that what I am doing by speaking out and dedicating my time to Holocaust education in Germany is right and must be done, not just for me, but for all future generations. I left his home feeling completely renewed and excited to continue this work. During my amazing trip back to Germany in 2010, my voice as a survivor has grown strong and is now resonating all over the world.

Dr. Stephan Wanner, mayor of Tutzing, has become a force for reconciliation and remembrance in Bavaria, formerly the center of the Nazi universe. I cannot thank him enough for the changes he has personally brought about in my life, in this case, through his tireless efforts to create a memorial to the victims of the Mühldorf death train, which eventually stopped in Tutzing on April 29, 1945. Back in Germany for another summer, my life's journey reached a milestone in September 2011 at the official ceremony for that memorial.

The Tutzing memorial means that there were indeed witnesses to what we went through, and in the end, hate did not triumph. Though the Nazis sought to destroy our heritage and remove the record of our contributions to society, they did not succeed. All the loneliness and isolation I felt has now been transformed into connection and community.

A stone monument erected in a Catholic cemetery at Tutzing is dedicated to the fifty-four prisoners who were murdered when the train stopped at Poing.

The monument reads "a sign of the inviolability of human dignity." Originally, only seventeen names were known out of the fifty-four, but seven more have been discovered by researchers.

If anything, the story of the fifty-four previously lost souls is also my story, for though I survived the train with my gunshot wound and typhus, the great hope I have lived to experience is that all the lost will one day be remembered. Their remains were exhumed from a graveyard near Dachau and moved to Tutzing where they were given a proper burial. The same spirit that lived in the Germans who helped me during the war is alive in so many Germans today, people like Dr. Wanner and Henry Mayer, and countless others who keep the memories alive.

The SS had hoped the death train would completely erase the last of the Hungarian Jews who had managed to survive the camps, but the failure of the Nazi Final Solution could not be more apparent today – finally and definitively the Nazi propaganda that had previously become so ingrained in my consciousness as a boy has been refuted. What the Nazis tried so hard to destroy lives on. I know who I am.

Though I broke down when I first told the story of my life for the archives at Dachau, I've been made strong by speaking out and going public with my story in Germany during the last two years. I am strong enough now to talk about anything. The inner voice that had always guided me is once again clear and vibrant – and now in complete harmony with my speaking voice.

Dr. Wanner calls the memorial a "posthumous contribution of integration and reconciliation" and that the memorial stone would contribute to a "living memorial culture." The inscription on the stone reads: "Open thy mouth for the dumb in the cause of all that are left." The speech preceding mine, given by Dr. Wanner, focused on the people who remain nameless; he said the memorial "reminds us again to respect the sanctity of human dignity"

The Central Council of Jews in Germany as well as the Catholic and Evangelical Church in Tutzing sponsored the event. Dr. Wanner spoke of the memorial service as a "clear sign of democracy, rule of law and tolerance and explained a clear, unambiguous and unequivocal rejection of any form of racism and xenophobia."

With Dr. Wanner looking on, my wife Annette, and my friend Max Mannheimer seated nearby, I delivered the keynote speech for the memorial service on Friday September 23, 2011:

Sixty-six years ago, during the spring and summer of 1945, World War II was ending. The worst armed conflict in human history was soon to be finished. Virtually no single person on the planet was left untouched by this tragedy.

The war took my family away from me – my mother, sisters, and step-father vanished right in front of my eyes at Auschwitz. Except for my nickname, Lazarus, I no longer even had a name. I was only a political prisoner as referenced by a red number – 71253.

I no longer had citizenship in my native Hungary or any other country for that matter. I had no papers and no passport. I owned nothing. I was fifteen years old.

At least three times I was supposed to die. In fact, I was barely recognizable as a living person – weighing less than 80 pounds with an open wound in my face. My jaw had been crushed when I was shot through the neck by a member of the Hitler Youth during the "Massacre at Poing" on April 27, 1945.

Max Mannheimer, my fellow survivor and world-renown educator and humanitarian, called my story "the biography of a child that survived Auschwitz and Dachau."

For nearly one year, I had indeed survived concentration camps and death trains. I survived beatings, starvation, and torture. I survived places where children simply didn't survive: Auschwitz, Dachau, Allach, Rotschweig, Mühldorf, Mettenheim, Poing, and finally my liberation at Tutzing.

Yet, Max Mannheimer also described me at this time, sixty-six years ago, as someone "on the edge of humanity" and "insensitive, cold, incapable of anything." The loneliness, fear, brutality, and constant hunger had indeed threatened to change me into something less than human.

Being here today on this solemn occasion again takes me back to the places of my worst humiliation and loneliness, but at the same time to a wondrous place in my mind.

You see there were three individuals who recognized and sought to heal the wounded child in me – Martin Fuss, Agnes Reisch, and Barbara Huber – and their spirit lives on today in the actions of their countrymen and women who seek reconciliation and healing.

Amid the most unspeakable acts of cruelty and horror ever committed by the human race, government to government and person to person, these three Germans looked into my eyes with compassion and love, and because of their actions, I knew somehow I would survive.

In the last few years, I have been following the path of Max Mannheimer. I have begun telling my story to young people in Germany and around the world. My book is now being published in English after previous versions in Danish and German. A documentary film has been made about my experiences.[4]

Everywhere I go people are eager to hear my story, and I cannot express how unimaginable all this would have been to me sixty-six years ago. My very presence here is a testament to my will to survive and to all the people who helped me.

My worst fear was that we would all simply disappear and no one would ever know what had happened to us. But we have not been forgotten.

My only wish now is for the world to know the peace and healing I have found. The kindness and compassion I have experienced from the people of modern Germany has amazed me; their search for truth and wisdom is also my search. The missing parts of my soul have been gathered together. I am made whole.

Picture 18: Leslie (center, seated) with German students, 2012.

---

4   *The Mühldorf Train of Death,* a film by Beatrice Sonhüter, debuted 30 April 2012 on Bavarian television in Germany; the film chronicles Leslie's experiences from 25-30 April 1945, including the Massacre at Poing and his liberation at Tutzing; all the events researched by students at the Franz-Marc School in Markt Schwaben guided by their teacher Henry Mayer. The teenagers are also featured in the film as they develop a relationship with Leslie.

Afterword: A Time of Healing

Marc David Bonagura

I first met Leslie Schwartz on November 9, 2010 after a talk he gave at the college where I teach. I sat in the back of a very crowded room but felt as if he were speaking only to me. He was surrounded by people waiting to greet him after his lecture, so I only had a chance to shake his hand and offer a quick word of thanks for coming.

I was so moved by his presentation that later that night I wrote a blog post expressing my admiration for his efforts and my interest in his message. My blog had previously been devoted to herbal medicine and had a small following, but after writing about Leslie, people from all over the world started reading it.

Many of the beliefs he discussed about the trauma and legacy of war resonated deeply with ideas I had developed from my work interviewing World War II veterans for the Library of Congress. Leslie called me a few weeks later one Sunday morning, and we have spoken almost every day since.

I first had no intention of writing a book with him, but as we became closer, he sent me the English translation of *Surviving Hell*, the Danish best seller about his life written with Karen Thisted. The English prose was powerful but rough. I felt if he had published that version, the impact of his message might have suffered in translation. More importantly, the healing he was undergoing had not yet been fully revealed to him or expressed in that manuscript. The additional two years we spent working on the book were entirely necessary.

All of Schwartz' words are very personal for me because my father, Michael J. Bonagura, fought in WWII, and his life was compromised in ways I'm only beginning to understand by the physical and emotional wounds he suffered during battles as a United States Marine against the Japanese in the Pacific.

Unlike Leslie, I simply cannot imagine my father ever wanting to return to Guadalcanal or revisit other former battle sites, and I couldn't really see him meeting with former Japanese soldiers either. I'll never know how completely my father made peace with the war, but I really feel compelled to do everything within my power to help Leslie continue his incredible journey. This work is in honor of my father's memory. One thing for sure, every day with Leslie is an adventure, something new and challenging on many different levels.

There is no more valuable study than the study of the Holocaust. Within that history is a microcosm of all human experience and relations. I believe we can learn from the past, but we also need to put that wisdom to good use. I am reminded of a few lines from a poem reflecting on the day the Nazis invaded Poland, "September 1, 1939" by W. H. Auden:

Hunger allows no choice
To the citizen or the police;
We must love one another or die.

Leslie has felt this hunger all his life. Now he feels love, especially from the German students who embrace his message, perhaps better able than past generations to face the complexity and lasting impact of that terrible time in history.

When individuals with sincere intentions get together, seeking healing through wholeness, with the strength and the desire to sit with whatever difficult and unsettling truths await them, they transform time into an instrument of healing rather than a trap that keeps reviving past trauma and conflicts, and they allow miracles to become everyday occurrences.

Before Hitler rose to power in 1933, there were approximately 500,000 Jews living in Germany. Many left before the war broke out; approximately 200,000 remained when the war started. Ninety per cent of those people were killed in the camps. In the 1990s, Russian Jews began immigrating to Germany, and now approximately 200,000 Jews again live in Germany – perhaps half that number remain active and visible in Jewish culture and religion. In a country of 80 million, one hundred thousand is a small number – so small that many Germans haven't ever met a Jew.

Leslie Schwartz and his fellow survivor Max Mannheimer are achieving unimaginable healing, while also creating a climate in which Jewish life can once again rise in Germany. They are developing a formula for conflict resolution that could benefit people everywhere.

Appendix A: Talking Weeds Blog
www.marcbonagura.blogspot.com

09 November 2010
Leslie Schwartz: Haftling Nummer 71253

I had the good fortune to attend an event sponsored by the Brookdale Center for World War II Studies and Conflict Resolution at Brookdale Community College in Lincroft, New Jersey: "Living Through Hell – an Evening with Leslie Schwartz" on Tuesday November 9, 2010.

After having attended the program and met with Mr. Schwartz afterward, I can only say he is an extraordinary human being, not even so much for his sufferings and survival at the hands of the Nazis in Auschwitz and Dachau, but for his lifelong quest for wholeness and his dedication to bear witness to the atrocities he experienced as a boy. This man is fearless.

Even as a teenager in the camps, he spoke of his strong will to survive: "The German press referred to me as *feisty* – I was determined that I must live, I must live that I can tell the horrible things that took place."

Schwartz continued, "I was with people in the concentration camps where they gave up; these people I had no feelings for – as a kid I always wanted to see people fighting." He calls this spirit "a Dachau thing in me."

He grew up in Hungary and told me his father was very strict in the old European traditions, and this tough upbringing helped make him strong.

The most significant aspect to his presentation is his search for healing. He has been a frequent traveler back to Germany in the years following the war, but his most recent trip was by far the most important as he traveled throughout Germany during the summer of 2010 speaking with high school students about his experiences. It seems the younger Germans are eager for history and are not afraid to face their ancestors' past. The feeling of honesty and truth seeking couldn't be more apparent from his anecdotes.

He described some of his experiences in "the new Germany" as he calls it as "nothing but glorious, glorious, [almost] unbearable." He went on, "I couldn't walk down the street – the kids hugged me." It was as if a dream had replaced the nightmares he's faced for more than sixty-five years.

He went on and on, "Is this possible? Is this Germany?" At one particular school he received ten minutes of applause from high school students, and of that experience he says, "my legs were shaking."

Leslie Schwartz is living proof that trauma from generations past can be healed if we are brave enough to revisit the source of the pain. There is no more optimistic news for those suffering from PTSD or other similarly related effects of war.

In all my years of interviewing WW II veterans, I have never come across a man so at peace with himself and so immersed in an aura of grace and healing. Leslie Schwartz is a hero to me in that he faced his fears by going back to the places where he was tormented and chose to revisit the people and descendents of the people who committed such unspeakable crimes – all the while doing so with compassion, not anger – not seeking revenge, only truth and wholeness.

He has gone on a quest to find the missing pieces of his soul, to gather them together in a way that benefits all that enter into his presence or read his story.

Although his feelings on God and religion are complicated, Schwartz is a holy man to me, a man who is able to look into the darkest realms of the human psyche with an unimaginable lightheartedness, wisdom, and even joy. He spoke of his move from Auschwitz to Dachau as if he were "moving into a country club – when you're tormented, you know the difference."

His understanding of a higher power has been a long, difficult process, but one he's not willing to forgo: "As you see all the horrible things, you question why? Why did I have to go through what I went through? For some reason I'm starting to believe that there is something."

Throughout the program all he could speak about was going back to Germany. He plans another trip in April 2011. He said, "I'm going back, looking forward to seeing those kids again." Schwartz has a book in print in Europe which is currently being translated into English and will be released sometime next year. [I had not yet been enlisted to work on the book.] To think he suffered all those years and within the last six months the many fragments of his soul have been gathered together is truly miraculous. Toward the end he offered, simply stated: "I'm kind of at peace with myself."

From my point of view, his journey could be summed up as follows: to bear witness to the evil that took place so the human race will never forget, to revisit the people and places and confront one's tormentors with a spirit of compassion and truth seeking in a quest for wholeness and peace, and to share his happiness and insight with the world. If Leslie Schwartz can find peace, there is hope for all of us. May the name Leslie Schwartz be forever spoken as a blessing.

05 February 2011
Leslie Schwartz Redux

"I wandered over the land, and good people did not neglect me. After many years I became old and white; I heard a great deal many lies and falsehoods, but the longer I lived the more I understood that there were really no lies. Whatever doesn't really happen is dreamed at night. It happens to one if it doesn't happen to another, tomorrow if not today, or a century hence if not next year."

-Isaac Bashevis Singer
"Gimpel the Fool"

Since my original post on Leslie Schwartz appeared in early November 2010, I have been in frequent contact with him. I recently had an opportunity to sit down with him in New York City to continue the conversation. Imagine, we sat and discussed the tragic events of sixty-six years past in complete comfort, dining at one of New York's finest restaurants, TBAR, run by a dear friend of Leslie's named Tony Fortuna. All we had to do is ask and anything we wanted would have appeared, as if magically, on that table. The restaurant was completely packed; smiling faces, people enjoying good food and conversation, and there I was taping his Holocaust stories of places like Dachau and Poing. Had Leslie been shown a vision of the future sixty-five years ago would he have believed it? Here he was eighty-one years old and at peace with all he's been through, surrounded by loved ones and admirers, eating fine food.

After interviewing him for more than four hours, I feel I've only scratched the surface. As one seeks to know Leslie and to understand the meaning of his extraordinary life, his words and deeds seem to exist out of time and space –

past, present, and future are all one. His gentle demeanor does not mask the clarity and intensity of his vision and his message.

I understand now that his words are teachings, important lessons for humans in this school called life. And people are hungry for this wisdom. There is no other way to explain his popularity; all ages are drawn to him wherever he goes. And Schwartz relates his experiences without self-aggrandizement or the force of his ego.

Martin Luther King often spoke of "soul force." The power of truth brought with compassion and love to overcome hate and bring about justice, peace, enlightenment – even transformation of the human race. Leslie is of a similar vibration.

I consider Leslie a veteran of the war though he never carried a weapon, and the only uniform he ever wore was a German one! In the early days after the war, he had no other clothes. His sometimes controversial story is about his fight for survival and human connection, a search for wholeness that would, like a latent seed, take sixty-five years to germinate, only breaking the ground toward heaven in the last year or so. In fact, Leslie has always been on this quest for wholeness. He jokingly refers to his constant desire to revisit these people and places as his personal form of "masochism." He simply has a soul that will not rest.

The Early Days after the War: The Search for Frau Riesch

After briefly returning to Hungary, he headed back to Germany. He was on a mission of sorts to reunite with Agnes Riesch. He recalls, "the first night we slept at the German museum, ice, ice-cold winter. The following day we went to the displaced persons camp. I was there for a while, and the most important thing was for me to go to find this lady, Agnes Riesch. When I came to her house, I rang the bell, and she recognized me. I would spend weekends in her house. She would cook, and I would bring food. She was to me like a mother. She referred to me as 'my son'. The name Lazarus came from there. She always called me Lazarus."

Frau Riesch had indeed left an indelible impression on young Leslie. In our recent interview he stated: "She saw me when I was in [the] concentration camp [at Dachau]. I had access to be alone, and she would pass through there with her bicycle, and I approached her – you know, do you have a piece of bread? And when she looked at me, [she thought] my gosh, what does a young kid like you do here? I was a political prisoner, and she couldn't figure this out – why I was a prisoner."

After their random meeting, she often brought him bread. First in secret and then openly in the face of the SS Guards. They told her if she kept it up, she'd be put in the camp, but in Schwartz' words, she said to the guards, "I don't care. I am old." They never touched her.

Leslie says, "the blessing for me was meeting this Frau Reisch, when I was in [the] concentration camp, and she brought me, every week, a piece of bread to eat, which they themselves did not have – emotionally, spiritually, it gave me immediately a feeling that here is a German lady who knew I was a Jew, yet she was so kind and helped me. I could not forget the people who were kind to me."

The Search for Barbara Huber in 2010

Frau Riesch wasn't the only German woman whom Leslie couldn't forget. In the last days of April 1945, Schwartz had been in Mühldorf with over five thousand prisoners, mostly Hungarian Jews who had earlier gone through Auschwitz. On April 25, 1945, 3,600 of them were loaded on a train to Tutzing, nick-named the death train. The train stopped in Poing, and there was an announcement that the war had ended. It would not end officially until May 8, 1945. The prisoners scattered, leaving the train for the town.

Leslie and a few others found a kind woman in a farmhouse in Poing who gave them food: "When I went to her farmhouse, she gave me a glass of milk, bread and butter." He recalls a crucifix hanging in her farmhouse and a comfortable feeling while in her home. She patted him on the head and cried, "You poor little boy," just like a mother. He thought to himself, "thank God, I am protected."

Later that day, someone he thought was an SS guard came to the door (actually a member of the Hitler Youth). When realizing the war had not ended, the SS Guards and others in the area came back and sought to round-up the prisoners to herd them back onto the death train.

The other boys with Leslie were able to hide, but Leslie thought he could outrun the Hitler Youth. He couldn't and the guard shot him in the head in the middle of a field in Bavaria. Schwartz was then told, "get up or I have to give you another bullet." Leslie was shot through the neck and jaw.

Leslie was then marched back to the death train. The dead and wounded were also put back onto the cattle cars. The events of this day became known as the Poing Massacre.

The train continued on toward Tutzing. Leslie never had any medical treatment. He could barely swallow and wondered if he would choke to death on his own saliva. Leslie somehow survived until the liberation by American GI's at Tutzing – the train's final destination. The pain he endured on that ride is almost unimaginable to him even today. He must have stayed conscious because he remembers the American bombers strafing the train cars on the passage to Tutzing. He thought, "the SS couldn't kill me, but the Americans might!"

As if all this weren't enough, he contracted Typhus in the days immediately following the German surrender and was sent to a hospital for Typhus patients. Again, he lived to tell about it, but was urged by an old friend of his father's who found him to seek treatment for his head wound that by that time had healed disfiguring his face. Reluctantly, Leslie went to a hospital where he was operated on by a former high-ranking Nazi surgeon who was also a master of reconstructive surgery. The recovery was the worst pain Schwartz had ever felt as the bones in his face had to be reshaped. Leslie was put in a hospital ward with all German soldiers who were also amputees – he was the only Jew there. He was still just fifteen years of age.

Leslie, however, was always driven to find the mystery woman who gave him the bread and milk. He recalled, "After the war, I went back to that village, and I could not find her. And this was an obsession with me; constantly, it bothered the hell out of me; why, why, why couldn't I find her? This past year when I went back, I made it a point." He continued, "when I went back [summer of 2010], I attended a birthday party, and I told one of the young men, 'George, do me a favor, I would like you to *Google* Poing. P-o-i-n-g – where I was shot' and this is how my whole story started."

Additionally, Leslie found his old friend Max Mannheimer through this search. Leslie hadn't seen Max in sixty-five years. Max was too weak to get off the train at Poing, as he had exhausted himself from an earlier attempt at escaping. Being reunited with Mannheimer has been another great blessing for Schwartz. Leslie added: "I met this Max Mannheimer, who is ninety years old – and he has received every conceivable award in Germany for what he's doing. For the past twenty-five years, he has visited 85,000 students, and this meeting with him, after sixty-five years, and knowing what he does; immediately, it gave me some ideas. You know, I think I should do this, too.

And I spoke to him about it, and that's how I was able to visit seventeen high schools; it was extremely rewarding for me, knowing that these kids are eager to listen to me and share my pain that I carried all these years."

Schwartz and Mannheimer were together in the camps and liberated together. Mannheimer is originally from Czechoslovakia. Just before the war ended, Leslie recalled Max telling him, if he ever survived, "'never again will I step foot on German soil,' but he met a German lady, fell in love, and has been there ever since!"

A freelance journalist named Otto Hartl accompanied Leslie throughout the trip. It was his article in the local paper that attracted the attention of Barbara Huber's daughter, Marianne Maier, who later found Leslie in a hotel and brought pictures of the farm where he drank that fateful glass of milk all those years ago.

Leslie Schwartz and Talking Weeds
07 February 2011

"I am a very strong believer that you never throw away people; you might put them on the side, but you never throw them away."
-Leslie Schwartz, New York City 2011

To reaffirm the theme of this blog and why Leslie Schwartz' story fits so well with it, one only need to look back to the title "Talking Weeds." Weeds are thought to have a less than desirable connotation and thereby something to be ignored or eradicated, yet the majority of the healing plants I know and use are considered weeds, especially Stinging Nettle.

Weeds can be used for food, healing, and even appreciated for their unique beauty, strength, and resiliency. We have an entire industry based on killing weeds, yet the weeds live on. How quickly and thoroughly this earth energy returns when we turn our backs on the open field for a few minutes! Sun, wind, and some rain, even just a little, and the weeds always return. Stop the cascade of pesticides for even a short time and the weeds return to the once "pristine" lawn.

Throughout history there have always been people the "dominant" group declares unfit or undesirable – or worse. World War II and the Holocaust are recent and blazing examples for all eternity of the end result of such thinking, elevated to a grand stage and given all the intention and energy possible by very creative and industrious peoples. That it took the collective efforts of the free world and sixty million lost lives to quell temporarily that energy only underscores how easy it is for large numbers of people to get on board that death train with their thoughts and deeds.

We take our shadow side and instead of embracing it project it onto other people and groups to demonize it and them, so we can eradicate it, always once and for all, even though the peace lasts only until the next war. Regarding disease and healing modalities, as well as politics and even religion, the same dualistic approach often guides the policymakers.

Think of all the "wars on – " something phrases put out there. War on cancer, drugs, terror, poverty, and so on. Fighting any war requires duality and the shadow of that which we wish to eradicate in ourselves, always projected onto the enemy of choice. The idea of embracing that shadow and thus making our "enemy" our ally, as my mentor Susun Weed says in her book *Healing Wise* is a complete change from the dualistic mentality still so prevalent in our current thinking.

As we strive to embrace all parts of our human experience, not throwing any of them away, but seeing what gifts even the darkest realms of our psyche may yield, we transform our lives. As we stop giving energy to the struggle we can't ever win, we have the opportunity to return to wholeness and to reclaim our tremendous power as individuals to manifest a wonderful, miraculous life – one in which we embrace more fully the gifts of Creation, while sharing our experience with others and helping them along their unique paths in life.

There is no other way to explain Leslie's story. Why would someone return (whether literally or in his mind), again and again, to the place of so much pain if not on a quest for wholeness? Think of the way in which Leslie embraced the small yet bold acts of kindness he experienced by just a few German people in the middle of one of the greatest nightmares in human history. This affirmation of humanity has been what has fueled his renaissance, and so many good things have happened to him since. The smallest acts of kindness and compassion sometimes hold the most power!

06 March 2011
In Honor of Dr. Halina Kustin Jagendorf & the Partisans of Vilna

"On its altar they gave the prime of their lives."
-Abba Kovner

Leslie Schwartz' dear friend, Dr. Halina Jagendorf, fought the Nazis when she was a teenager. She and her mother and brother were part of the famous Partisans of Vilna, fighting in the forests of Rudnitska, Lithuania. Dr. Jagendorf's mother, Dinah Mishcon Kustin, was a cook for the partisans. Halina served as a field nurse. They fought with the legendary resistance fighter Abba Kovner.

On July 13, 1944 the partisans, then united with the Soviet Army, liberated Vilna. The Nazis never could overcome them. Their resistance was critical to the allied efforts, and I don't believe they were ever given the credit they truly deserve. They were featured in a documentary film *Partisans of Vilna.*

Leslie has known Halina since his earliest days in the United States. At the time, 1947, Leslie was seventeen years of age. He attended Jefferson High school in the Brownsville section of Brooklyn; Halina and her brother Abe also attended the school for immigrants who did not speak English. Leslie told me there were about twenty holocaust survivors in that high school, and he recalled they all were able to communicate by speaking Yiddish (which he learned in the concentration camps). Leslie said he was very happy to go to high school, "I enjoyed what I missed as a fourteen year-old – that period I lost – I was reunited with kids."

At the time the two year age difference between Halina and Leslie, "like day and night" in Leslie's own words, sealed his fate; all he would ever be to her was "a kid." For a European woman, a younger man was not so attractive. Halina was a brilliant and beautiful older woman. What did Leslie have to offer her in those days?

They lost touch for many decades. Occasionally, Leslie would hear from her brother, Abe, who had left the US and moved to Israel. Abe used to chastise Leslie for staying in the US, always telling him his place was in Israel, but Leslie felt very connected to the US.

As the years passed by, there were many changes in both lives. Halina had married a prominent New York physician, and she herself earned a Doctorate in Psychotherapy and began a long, successful practice in New York City.

Leslie was only reunited with Halina a few years ago after receiving a wedding invitation to Abe's son's wedding in Israel. Abe told Leslie, "my sister would be happy to see you." Despite her immense professional success, Halina has gone through more than her share of hardship in this country; in fact, one could argue that her battles against the Nazis were nothing in comparison to the trials and tribulations she would endure later in life.

This kind of chaotic life is certainly not unusual for a combat veteran or Holocaust survivor; they often need to struggle mightily to keep their lives from completely unraveling, almost at regular intervals, as those waves of trapped energy (experiences from the war years locked within one's human form) regularly spiral outward, like squall bands from a hurricane, affecting everyone within close range of the survivor. This phenomenon is mostly invisible and undocumented but very real.

I saw this in my father's life and in so many others' lives. The war never truly ends for someone like Halina; its echoes always reverberating in strange and grotesque ways, a constant internal battle, like a war against the peace and prosperity of her new life in America – how could the chaos not return? Yet she always faced everything stoically and with honor, but by this point (2006-2007) in her life, the visit from Leslie, a happy face from the past, would bring her immeasurable comfort and joy.

Leslie is no longer an insignificant kid, but a loving presence from better days. Leslie tells me of their genuine affection for each other, their bonds forged in the horrors of war, and she has told Leslie "there are certain things I would not discuss with anyone but you." Halina suffered terribly during the war. She lived in the forest for years while fighting the Nazis, and she did everything she could to keep her family together, but her sacrifices were great. No teenager should have to go through what she did – just to survive. Interestingly, she often tells Leslie how she "would [still] love to be eighteen again."

Leslie tells me his relationship with Halina is one of the most important in his life, almost as if he feels responsible for keeping her spirit alive. They talk frequently, and when he is in New York, he visits her quite often. Now, her health is failing, and she is mostly confined to a wheelchair; she lives with her husband (who suffers from Alzheimer's Disease) and daughter Lorri.[5]

Leslie really feels a part of their family. He said, "the whole thing really affects a guy like me." Leslie vowed to Halina, "You will never walk the last road alone."

---

[5] Halina's story, "My Mother Halina Kustin Jagendorf, Partisan," by Lorri A. Jagendorf is featured on page 382 in *Anthology on Armed Jewish Resistance 1939-1945 Volume II* by Isaac Kowalski.

Appendix B: Selected Lectures to Students

The first lecture was given by Leslie Schwartz on February 27, 2011 to six and seventh graders at reformed Temple Sinai in Delray Beach, Florida, and later at Central Synagogue in New York City on April 12, 2011. The second address is typical of Leslie's speech to secondary students in Germany; it also serves as the introduction to the documentary film *The Mühldorf Train of Death* (2012) by Beatrice Sonhüter.

If you were to see me walking down the street, would you know what I have gone through?

Quite naturally, all teenagers struggle to some degree with their identity. The basic questions of who am I? What is my life to be about? What is really important to me, and how do I go about finding and then expressing the true nature of my intellect, talents, and spirituality in the healthiest and most productive manner?

How does my particular faith and my understanding of its traditions and responsibilities relate to my choices and decisions that while made presently will also affect the rest of my life?

At the age of thirteen, I faced incredible challenges to my sense of self, my purpose in life, and, of course, the expression of my Jewish faith. My thirteenth year marked a true coming-of-age into manhood, just as the traditional Bar Mitzvah suggests. In fact, it was the beginning of my journey through hell and back. I believe my message is especially relevant for all of you – you who were blessed with the gift of being born and growing up in America. My hope is that you will not take your opportunities for granted.

At thirteen, I was first uprooted from my village in Hungary, and my family was sent to the Hungarian/Ukrainian border, for all practical purposes, to be eliminated by the Nazis and Hungarian Nazi sympathizers (of which there were no shortage). The premise for the destruction – as Jews, we were not Hungarian citizens anymore. Although my great grandparents were born in Hungary, the questioning of our citizenship was the first great lie spread to dehumanize and isolate the Jews of my village.

My family and I were shipped to the mountains on the border of Hungary and Ukraine, a beautiful region actually, to be killed right then and there, but the advancing Russian troops necessitated that we be sent back to our village again.

Upon returning, my village wasn't the same. Life had been transformed by the war and conditions were terrible – the Nazis had taken everything. I remember the Jewish storekeepers opening their stores; it was a free for all with everyone running around and taking whatever they wanted.

As much as a rebellious teenager might find this chaos appealing on some level, I knew everything was all wrong. The Nazi propaganda was also starting to take hold on my psyche. My mind was poisoned, and I began to accept my own "inferiority."

Once home again in my village, I was forced to attend a Catholic school, and it was there I fell in love with a young Catholic girl named Judith; she was also the daughter of my teacher. She told me, "my parents don't want me to look at you." Her parents were both school teachers, the intellectual elite of the village; whether they had bought into the Nazi lies or were just trying to survive themselves, there would be no sympathy for me.

But not everything in my story is about the Holocaust. The love and confusion of a young boy knew no boundaries, and I thought of Judith for many years afterward, finally to see her again in 1995. The reunion was the ending of a great love in sadness, as old age and infirmity had taken their toll on her. Her family later suffered their own tragedies at the hands of the Communists – Judith's brother was imprisoned for fifteen years before escaping to live in France, another betrayal at the hands of one's own countrymen.

Although the concentration camps were kept secret and no one knew what was to come at Auschwitz and Dachau, the complete thoroughness of the abandonment and betrayal of the Hungarian Jews, who had been such a vital part of the fabric of life in Hungary, is still difficult for me to imagine.

Just before being sent to Auschwitz, I remember vividly two young SS Guards in the Ghetto, just teenagers themselves, impressively dressed in their SS uniforms with their German shepherd dogs, not unlike the dog I loved and left behind in my village. What was so different about these teenagers? Did they not breathe the same air? The uniforms, the lies, the terror, the brutality, and even the sheer power of the military-industrial machine of the Nazi empire were not enough in the end to defeat me. I survived to tell my story; they did not.

Remember, one's perceptions of strength and weakness, superiority and inferiority, are not always accurate, so don't always trust the impressions of what the world around you considers powerful and valuable–not at thirteen, nor at any age. Rather, place your trust in the human spirit – universal, yearning for freedom, and for the expression of beauty, love, and truth.

Next time you feel your lives are too difficult, think of my story and realize the many blessings you have been given to have been born in America.

To German Secondary Students:

Martin Luther King Jr. once wrote, "We are not makers of history. We are made by history." Truer words about my life have not been spoken.

Each and every Holocaust survivor must come to terms with the concept of loss. The losses we suffered are so vast and unfathomable that I believe it takes a long lifetime to confront them and perhaps many generations to heal them.

I was only a young boy when the troubles in my country began, and at four-teen years of age, I lost my freedom, my family, my citizenship, my identity, and even my name. But above all these very real and tangible losses I suffered, the worst loss of all is simply being forgotten.

To be removed and isolated from all aspects previously associated with being human and all activities historically and traditionally associated with hu-manity – to realize the enemy has taken you away from any future opportunity for joy and nurturing human relations is the most tragic loss of all. You become a ghost, human only in your biology. Your awareness and consciousness is no longer among the living. You exist to pass time only until, quite literally, you join the ghostly realm.

And while you're passing time in hell, you're barely able to associate with the other ghosts who, just like you, are ready to let go of everything good that makes us human and connected to each other. In this condition you can very easily just give up; this was never my choice, but it is the real war a survivor like me had to fight everyday in the camps and for decades afterwards.

Now understand that what I am about to say is a very radical statement – but my captors also became ghosts – for they also had to abandon their humanity as well, and when a nation creates a war machine and becomes the perpetrator of such inhuman crimes, the nation itself risks losing its humanity.

One may be on the "free" side of the fences or camp walls, but that freedom is illusory – to bind others one must also be bound. In this way I can completely relate to and understand why my search for healing is also Germany's search for healing. We're not separate in this process.

Some people think it strange for a Holocaust survivor to have embraced this healing initiative in Germany, but I do not. It seemed to me, right from the first days after the war until today, the only possible option. My healing is forever linked with Germany's healing.

That's why I could not be happier about the documentary you are about to see. Beatrice Sonhüter has captured the essence of my struggles and the profound healing journey I have also traveled, leading right up to our conversation today.

And for me to speak to you today is of course an honor, but it is also unimaginable – because if you were to see me at age fourteen, being taken away with my family in a cattle wagon headed for Auschwitz – well, not only did I think I might never return to my village of Baktalórántháza in Hungary, but I wondered if I would ever return to the place of the living, much less become a man who would one day speak to people who might actually want to hear what he has to say.

The Nazi's began to carry out their final solution in Hungary in 1944, and by the time the smoke had cleared, over 500,000 Hungarian Jews (from 800,000 who lived there before the war) would be murdered, including my mother, sisters, and stepfather, so the odds were against me to say the least. In fact, at least three times before the age of sixteen, I should have died. I have been imprisoned, brutalized, starved, slaved, and shot.

So, there is no logical or plausible explanation as to why I stand here before you, except for the miraculous and defiant acts of kindness by a few people I encountered during my time in the camps – people who also happen to be German. And I would not be here today without them. Small acts of love often hold the greatest power.

And this is the wonderful and the challenging part of my story – as a teenage survivor of Auschwitz, Dachau, and other sub-camps of Dachau, including Mühldorf and the death train I was forced to ride in the last days of the war (you will soon learn much more about this from the documentary), one would think that I have nothing but hatred for Germany and the German people, and that might have been the case if not for these three particular Germans who defied the Nazi hatred with unbelievable kindness: Martin Fuss, Agnes Reisch, and Barbra Huber.

Martin Fuss offered me encouragement, friendship, and liverwurst sandwiches when I worked at the railroad station in Karlsfeld near Allach.

Agnes Reisch gave me bread, money, and her food vouchers in Dachau – she called me "Dear son, Lazarus" – in complete defiance of the SS Guards I might add. They told her, "if you keep this up, we'll put you in here." She told them, "I don't care, I'm old." They never touched her by the way.

And Barbara Huber, from the kitchen of her small farmhouse in Bavaria, reached out to me and three other ghostly survivors, nothing but skin and bones, barely alive, who had fled the death train during the Poing Massacre serving us the most delicious bread, butter and milk I have ever tasted.

Barbara Huber, like Agnes Reisch before her, considered me her son – an emaciated, half-dead, teenage, Jewish, concentration camp prisoner was also *her son.* I did not learn Barbara Huber's name for more than sixty-five years, but she, Martin Fuss, and Agnes Reisch never left my memory for one day.

All the miraculous events that have occurred in my life in the past few years have been a direct result of my search for Barbara Huber. Through a series of newspaper stories in Germany during the summer of 2011, I was able to meet her daughter Marianne Meier, and thus begin my journey which has brought me to you today.

All three helped to save more than just my body, for nourishment is more than food, but thoughts and feelings too – and most importantly, they helped keep me from the Nazi mindset of hatred.

You see when you are oppressed and put in that position of being on the receiving end, quite literally, of genocide, it is very easy to hate the people that did this to you, and many people would say that hatred was entirely justified, even necessary to be returned in kind, but for me that was not the case because three kind Germans put seeds of hope in my mind and love in my heart, showing me that all Germans were not the same.

That was a good lesson to learn because it would prove very valuable to me during my life-long search for wholeness – and good advice for those interested in facilitating the healing that needs to take place among all people on this planet for so many other, perhaps less well known, but no less horrible atrocities we humans keep inflicting upon each other in the sixty-seven years since WW II ended.

I've learned that only love can conquer hatred, but love, let me remind you, serves us better as a verb rather than a noun – to say, to think, to wish love is good – but to act, to feel, and to experience love is better.

Because I can tell you, when you rescue the heart of a child (just as my heart was rescued all those years ago) in any similarly desperate circumstances, you save the life of the adult who will then carry for the rest of his or her life, instead of a message of hate, a message of love – and one that will resonate and touch many other lives.

In the last few years, I have come together with so many people from all over the world for whom my story has found powerful resonance. And there has been no greater happiness and healing for me to experience than the love of young people who can relate to my story, especially the German students I have spoken with for the last two years as an honored guest in the country that once sought to exterminate me – yes, now I'm honored, respected, acknowledged, loved, and definitely not forgotten – this is the unimaginable miracle that has made me whole.

So now you are about to see a documentary film that chronicles a short period during the last days of my imprisonment, but the one message I want you to walk away with, which is my life's message, is no matter what, healing and wholeness are always possible.

We no longer need to pretend we're all separate – we can indeed face the sometimes brutal but also beautiful greater reality that we are all connected. And that freedom from hatred truly is possible.

Appendix C: Holocaust Memorial Day

Otto Rona[6]

The Holocaust has been the largest organized massacre in the history of mankind. A crime committed by a distorted, inhuman ideology, mean instincts, and guided by practical interests. It highlighted how fragile humanism is and how weak morals and human dignity are.

It is almost incomprehensible that [the] Holocaust has actually taken place. We should keep it forever in our memories and learn the necessary lessons from it. There are all kinds of memorial days on almost every day of the year. We do not know the substance of most of them. The Holocaust Memorial Day could fall on actually any day of the year as the nightmare dragged on throughout more than an entire decade. The memory of our eradicated and humiliated brothers and sisters stays with us. Nobody and nothing is to be forgotten.

Many people know – although many of them very much want to forget, and worse yet, some want to make others forget – that the Nazis and their European accomplices murdered six million Jews during the Second World War. They employed various methods – hunger, beating, hanging, shooting, and gassing. Nearly one tenth of the victims were Hungarian Jews, which means 550,000 people.

Even the definition is strange: a "Hungarian Jew." A major element constituting the tragedy of the Jews in Hungary was that those people who after their Emancipation (1867) became unreservedly Hungarians regarding their language, customs, clothing, and most importantly, their feelings were excluded from the community of Hungarian citizens.

---

[6] Otto Rona is the former Hungarian Ambassador to Denmark. He delivered this address at the Holocaust Memorial Day luncheon in Copenhagen, Denmark on January 26, 2007 in honor of the publication *Overleve Helvede* or *Surviving Hell,* Leslie Schwartz' story written with Karen Thisted. This event was sponsored by Lars Henrik Munch, CEO JP/Politikens Hus, one of Denmark's leading media companies.

Governor Horthy's regime (1920-1944) carried out their gradual exclusion by a series of Jewish Laws passed after 1938. Those very same Jews, about whom Theodor Herzl stated with resignation at the turn of the century that they became a "dry bough" of Zionism, suddenly realized that their homeland, for which they had fought for with such a devotion during the First World War (more than ten thousand Hungarian Jews died and thousands upon thousands were wounded and disabled), regards them as alien enemies. This was the case in spite of the fact that the overwhelming majority of the Hungarian Jewry, notwithstanding the orthodoxim, regarded themselves as Hungarians following the "faith of Moses."

The abovementioned anti-Semite laws completed the exclusion of the Hungarian Jews between 1938 and 1941. The first two laws made their economic situation more and more difficult, the Third Jewish Law, which was passed in 1941, however, was a real Nuremberg-type, racial law introducing "raceprotective" orders.

In July and August 1941, nearly 16,000 Jews, regarded as aliens or whose citizenship was stated to be unresolved, were deported to territories under German rule in Galicia where the Germans massacred them in the vicinity of Kamenec-Podolskij. This was the first "five-digit" massacre during the process of the Holocaust of the European Jewry.

In the spring and early summer of 1944, Eichmann and his SS-Sonderkommando of two-hundred men deported the Jews of the Hungarian provinces to Auschwitz with the active help of the Hungarian clerks, policemen, soldiers and gendarmeries. The Jewry of the provinces, 437,000 people, made up more than fifty percent of the entire Hungarian Jewry.

Miklós Horthy however put an end to the deportations on 6 July 1944. The reasons are still not entirely clear. It is possibly that his decision was motivated by the landing of the allied forces on the shores of Normandy or the offensive of the Red Army or he was afraid that the capital would have been destroyed by a carpet bombing if the Jews of Budapest had been deported. Eichmann was unable to continue shipping "raw material" to the death factory of Auschwitz without help from the Hungarian authorities.

Ferenc Szálasi, the leader of the Arrow-Cross Party and the Hungarist Movement came to power with the help of the Germans after Miklós Horthy, the governor of Hungary, appealed for cease-fire with the allied forces. Nearly 200,000 Jews were terrified by the coming to power of Szálasi's Arrow-Cross men. The troops of the Red Army were unable to liberate the ghetto of Budapest until 18 January 1945. Up to then, hundreds of defenseless Jews were murdered by Arrow-Cross men every day. Many Jews were tortured horribly before their death, others simply shot and thrown into the ice-covered water of the Danube. They handed over nearly 70,000 Jews to the Germans for forced labour. They worked on the fortification system in the Sub-Alps in order to "protect" Vienna.

In the spring of 1945, Budapest was reduced to ruins. As a result of the meaningless war fought on the Nazis' side, nearly one million lives were lost. From 825,000 Hungarian Jews 550,000 died, and some of the returning survivors emigrated within the next few years. Thus, in the place where one of the most flourishing Jewish communities of Central-Eastern Europe once existed, now approximately 100,000 Jews live.

The Nobel Prize in literature won in 2002 by the Hungarian-Jewish Holocaust survivor Imre Kertész proves that the memories of the Holocaust should be preserved for future generations, and I commend the work of Leslie Schwartz as a strong message for the future as well.

Leslie Schwartz

Leslie Schwartz
Durch die Hölle von Auschwitz und Dachau
Ein Junge erkämpft sein Überleben
„Ich sollte nicht leben.
Es ist ein Fehler. Ich wurde am 12. Januar 1930 geboren.
Ich bin ein Jude. Dreimal schon sollte der Tod mich ereilt haben.
Die Gründe, warum ich die Hölle überlebt habe, sind in dem Verlangen zu sehen, meine Geschichte zu erzählen. Ich hatte Alpträume. Ich dachte, wir alle wären tot und ich könnte nichts berichten. Dann hätte niemand von den Ereignissen erfahren.
Nun bin ich 80. Mein Name ist Leslie Schwartz.
Wenn ich meine Geschichte erzählen will, so muss es jetzt sein, jetzt bleibt mir noch Zeit."
(Leslie Schwartz)
Anpassung – Selbstbehauptung – Widerstand, Bd. 29, 2010, 120 S., 16,90 €, br., ISBN 978-3-643-10821-0

LIT Verlag Berlin – Münster – Wien – Zürich – London
Auslieferung Deutschland / Österreich / Schweiz: siehe Impressumsseite